The Masterpieces of the
OHIO MOUND BUILDERS

The Masterpieces of the OHIO MOUND BUILDERS

THE HILLTOP FORTIFICATIONS INCLUDING FORT ANCIENT

E. O. Randall

COMMONWEALTH BOOK COMPANY
St. Martin, Ohio

Originally published by the
Ohio Archaeological and Historical Society in 1908.

This edition Copyright © 2023 by
Commonwealth Book Company, Inc.

All rights reserved. No part of this book may be reproduced in any form or by any means without the prior written consent of the publisher, excepting brief quotes used in reviews.
Printed in the United States of America.

ISBN: 978-1-948986-60-1

COVER IMAGE: Serpent Mound, Adams County
TITLE PAGE IMAGE: Fort Hill, Highland County

PREFATORY NOTE.

THIS little volume makes no pretense of being a scientific or technical treatise on the Ohio Mound Builders or their works. Its aim is to briefly describe the chief relics of the Ohio Mound Builders as they now appear, and as they appeared when found in their original condition, or when first studied by archaeological students. Some twelve years ago the author became the Secretary of the Ohio State Archaeological and Historical Society. The duties of his office were confined to the executive affairs of the Society and the work of the Society along its historical lines. The archaeological department has been in the care of specialists in that subject. Professor G. Frederick Wright, Warren K. Moorehead, Gerard Fowke, Professor W. C. Mills and others connected with the Society have given their attention to the prehistoric researches and have produced many valuable publications as the result of their investigations. The author of the pages herewith issued naturally came in contact with the work of these scholars and acquired an irresistible interest in the subject — a subject fraught with fascination because of its uniqueness and mystery. The author has visited all the earthen works herein described — some of them many times — so that the descriptions are those of first hand, "views taken on the spot." This volume is confined to the Hilltop Fortifications. The author hopes at no distant day to supplement these studies with descriptions of the chief Lowland Enclosures, Mounds and Village sites. The so-called great religious relic of these lost people, known as Serpent Mound, has been minutely treated by the author in a volume recently published by the Society.

E. O. RANDALL.

February, 1908.

CAHOKIA MOUND.

During a sojourn in that fairyland of modern marvels, the Louisiana Purchase Exposition, held at St. Louis, in the summer of 1904, it was the privilege of the writer in company with a party includ-

Cahokia Mound as Originally Appearing.

ing several students of American Archæology, to make an inspection of the world-famed Cahokia Mound. We crossed the sweeping Mississippi to the Illinois side, over the colossal bridge, one of the engineering achievements of modern invention and skill, which, had it existed in the ancient days of oriental glory, would have been regarded, if not the first, then easily the eighth wonder of the world. A half hour's ride on a swift speeding trolley car bore us inland some six miles, landing us almost at the base of the great mound — called respectively "Cahokia Mound," from the Indian tribe which formerly inhabited the locality, and the "Monks' Mound," from the fact that in the year 1810 a colony of Trappists settled thereabouts and occupied a monastic building, which they erected on the summit of the mound. After only a few years' sojourn, the solitude seeking religionists returned to France. But little evidence remains of their occupancy.

The Mound Builders never failed to exercise sagacious judgment in their choice of sites for habitation or the erection of their chief structures. No better place could have been found for the Cahokia and its surrounding mounds than in the upper Mississippi valley near the juncture of the Missouri from the West and the Illinois from the Northeast, a strategetical point on the main waterways of the vast Northwest. For many miles below the mouth of the Missouri, the east side of the Mississippi broadens into a plain some eight or ten miles in width, interrupted by a line of bluffs which form its eastern boundary. This stretch of level surface composed of rich, fertile, alluvial deposit is known as the "American Bottom." Several creeks cross it from its eastern limit to the Mississippi and many little lakes formerly dotted the thick growths of timber and prolific underbrush that in the early days must have clothed it. This was a prime hunting territory for fish, fowl and game, well adapted to the primitive life of a prehistoric people. Near the center of this bottom and just south of its chief stream, the Cahokia stands to-day, as it has stood for untold centuries, the most massive and imposing monument of the Mound Builders in this country and probably in the world. Surrounding this mound, within a radius of two or three miles, in a more or less perfect state of preservation, in varying shapes and sizes, from ten to sixty feet in height, are some fifty lesser mounds. At still greater distances from the center structure, in groups or isolated examples, are many more. Great numbers have been obliterated. Doubtless in the days of the "Golden Era" of the Mound Builder, hundreds of mounds dotted the American Bottom. Scores of these strange earth-heaps originally occupied the site of St. Louis and were demolished to make way for the lengthening streets and spreading squares of that metropolis. On these banks of the mighty river must have been a vast population whose labors were almost incredible in their results as evidenced by the relics still extant.

Cahokia Mound is a truncated rectangular pyramid, rising to a height of one hundred feet above the original surface upon which it was built. The dimensions of its base are: from north to south, 1,080 feet; from east to west, 710 feet. The area of the base is therefore something over sixteen acres. This is a greater area than the base of the Pyramid of Cheops — the greatest of the Egyptian tombs. The size may be better understood when compared with the State House square in Columbus, which measuring from fence to fence is ten acres in space; taking in the width of the four surrounding streets gives nearly the area of the great mound. The mound was

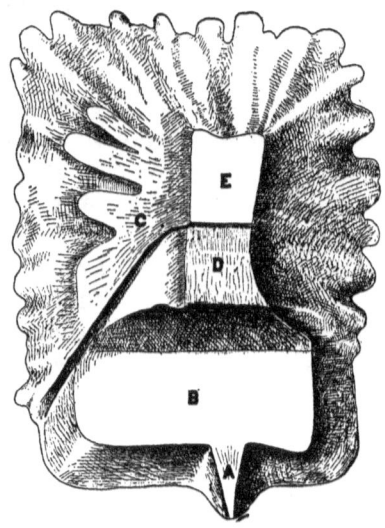

Plan of Cahokia Mound from Above, Showing Worn Sides.

originally a curious series of receding terraces, four in number. The peculiar design will be better understood by the accompanying illustrations, than by any attempted verbal description.

In the plan representing the structure as appearing when viewed from above, the lowest terrace (B) extends 500 feet from east to west and 200 feet from north to south. From the south face of that terrace, a point (A) having the appearance of a graded approach, prospects due south from a distance of about eighty feet. The second terrace (C) is at the present time badly gutted and worn away, which makes it difficult to ascertain the exact size or elevation. The next terrace (D) has an elevation of ninety-seven feet above the original mound base surface. Near the center of this terrace there formerly stood a small conical mound, long since destroyed. The fourth terrace (E) is now the most elevated platform of the mound. Its greatest height is one hundred feet above the plain or three feet above the third terrace; it was probably higher in its pristine condition. The area of this summit terrace is about 200 by 160 feet. The dark line on the left of the mound, leading from the base to the summit, is a modern pathway for easy ascent. The contents of this mound have been estimated to considerably exceed one million cubic yards of earth; and the labor of loading and unloading this material or carrying it from a likely distance would occupy 2,500 men two years, working every day in the year. There is little dispute among scientists concerning the conclusion that this is an artificial mound. Those who have made geological demonstrations and archæological explorations have generally agreed that this enormous pile of earth was built by a primitive and prehistoric people and, so far as any evidence can be shown,

6   *Masterpieces of the Mound Builders.*

built by hands with implements of the crudest and most primitive character. There are, however, not-

Cahokia Mound — East Side.

able exceptions to this agreement. Professor Daniel G. Brinton, formerly of the Pennsylvania University

Cahokia Mound — West Side.

and one of the most distinguished Americanists of this country, says: "It is doubtful whether this (mound) is wholly an artificial construction," and he cites Professor Spencer Smith as saying it is "largely a natural formation." There are always skeptics no matter how overwhelming the proof.

This truncated, terraced form of mound had its analogy in many of the temples of Mexico and Central America and indeed in many of the early works of oriental nations. Such is the monarch, man-made mountain as it was raised above the plain in the midst of this Mound Builders' country.

The first view, to the archæological student, is apt to be dispelling of a preconceived idea, which is usually that of the mound in its architectural prime. Its original clear cut lines and arithmetical proportions are blunted by the wear of age. Deep furrows have marred its sides and wrinkled its front. Though resisting valiantly, it has bowed to the storms of nature and the vandal assaults of civilized man.

We climbed the jagged flank to the summit and stood upon the elevation that lifted us above the surrounding plain. It was an amiable afternoon in September; the sun had crossed the Mississippi, and well on his way to the western horizon, cast a mellow tone over the landscape that lay before us. The broad valley gave us a peaceful and pleasing view—stretching to the east till cut off by the dim outline of the uplands; to the west to the great "Father of Waters" which like an irresistible flood plowed its way to the Mexican Gulf. Round about on every hand, like contrasting features of a race vanished and forgotten and a people now world predominant, were interspersed the weather beaten and depleted mounds and the prosperous farm homes. In many instances these homes were built on the mounds, typifying the conquest of civilization over savagery, the inevitable survival of the fittest. It was a scene for the historian and the philosopher, the artist and the poet. As one writer observes: "There was a double presence which was forced upon the mind — the presence of those who since the beginning of historic times have visited the region and gazed upon this very monument and written descriptions of it, one after the other, until a volume of literature has accumulated; and the presence of those who in prehistoric times filled the valley with their works, but were unable to make any record of themselves except such as is contained in these silent witnesses." Here certainly was one of the great centers, if not the chief center, in the western continent of this myterious people. Many writers and students conclude that if the Mound Builders of the territory now embraced in the United States had a central government, it must from all evidences, have been located here in the American Bottom of the Mississippi valley. Here in greatest number were found their largest monuments, which bear testimony to their patience and industry and long sojourn. In the mounds and in the intervening fields were found astonishing quantities of human bones, and crude stone implements of war and of domestic life, simple but eloquent witnesses of the most primitive stage of human progress. No copper or iron artifacts were found. These people had never emerged from the age of stone — the rocky road of life.

And was this gigantic earthen structure their temple, their religious tabernacle, the "great central shrine of the Mound Builders' empire," "upon which," suggests one writer and distinguished scholar, "one hundred feet above the plain, were their sanctuaries, glittering with barbaric splendor and where could be seen from afar the smoke and flames of the eternal fire, their emblem of the sun."

"This mound stands," writes Professor Stephen D. Peet, "like a solemn monarch, lonely in its grandeur, but imposing in its presence. Though the smoke of the great city may be seen in the distance and many trains go rumbling across the valley and through the great bridge which spans the river, yet this monster stands as a mute witness of a people which has passed away. It is a silent statute, a sphinx, which still keeps within its depths the mystery which no one has yet fathomed. It perpetuates the riddle of the sphinx."

Was it some mighty tomb erected to be the fitting mausoleum of a great conqueror or chief — some terrible Attila, or invincible Alaric, a Caesar or Napoleon of savage days? Small wonder that the scene presented from that Cahokia summit awakened one's curiosity and stirred one's imagination. Marvelous relic — preservation of a prehistoric people, looming like the dome of a cathedral from the level valley — the arena in which a vast race had lived and toiled, had come, seen and perhaps had conquered, achieved their ambitions and proudly expended their energies. A race of mystery, whence and when it came, whither or when it went, no man knoweth unto this day. All is locked in impenetrable secrecy. As my companions were discussing the unsolved riddle of the past, there came to our memory Volney's Meditations on the "Ruins of Empires;" — seated amid the demolished architectural splendors of Palmyra in the Syrian plain of the historic Euphrates, there passed before his "mind's eye" the representatives of buried dynasties and dead faiths. What a chance was here at Cahokia for some historico-philosophic dreamer "to interrogate ancient monuments on the wisdom of past times." Surely here were the remains of a vast and vanished empire. In this valley of the Mississippi had flourished, who knows how long ago, a mighty nation; they had builded better than they knew, for their simple and stupendous structures had survived "the tooth of time and razure of oblivion."

The Mound Builder had certainly founded his kingdom; it had flourished, for he had erected imperishable and inscrutable memorials; imposing structures that survived ages and races. Could some wizard's wand recall the procession of the people who had made their entrees and their exits in this Mississippi valley, what a varied and graphic panorama would be unfolded! The Mound Builders had dwelt here in great numbers and power for generations, only to join "the innumerable caravan that moves to that mysterious realm" which is the destiny of races as of men; then came at least one other savage successor, the child of the forest, the Indian; bitter and bloody was the struggle of his stay, but his happy hunting grounds were to be the dwelling place of the pale

Original Cahokia Mound.

face. Yes, even the white intruder, the European usurper, had made this American Bottom memorable; it had been the field of the national contest for supremacy in the Western World; in turn the Spaniard, the Frenchman, the Briton and the American had struggled for this winning of the West; here DeSoto and his gaily attired cavaliers had planted the flag of Castile and Aragon; here the Jesuit priest and the adventurous *couriers de bois* had sought favor with the redmen and claimed the basin of the Mississippi for La Belle France; here the insatiable Anglo-Saxon had supplanted the banner of the Bourbons with the standard of St. George and the Dragon; and here that patriotic and dauntless "Washington of the West," Colonel George Rogers Clark and his heroic little band of Virginia riflemen had carried in triumph the Stars and Stripes and saved the Northwest Territory to the infant republic; and now "last scene of all that ends this strange eventful history," the peaceful homes of the American farmer crown the summits of the temples of the Mound Builders. Is this the final chapter or are others yet to be written? Macauley, in his famous prophecy, wrote: "She (Rome) saw the commencement of all the governments and of all the ecclesiastical establishments that now exist in the world; and we feel no assurance that she is not destined to see the end of them all. She was great and respected before the Saxon had set foot on Britain, — before the French had passed the Rhine, — when Grecian eloquence still flourished at Antioch, — when idols were still worshipped in the temple of Mecca. And she may still exist in undiminished vigor when some traveller from New Zealand shall, in the midst of a vast solitude, take his stand on a broken arch of London Bridge to sketch the ruins of St. Paul."

So the Mound Builder was here before European civilization found its foothold on the Western Continent, and his relics have survived centuries of civilized conflict; perhaps a cycle hence some representative of another race yet unborn, the ultimate racial composite man, may stand upon the summit of Cahokia and as he wonders over its age and origin may look about him and witness the ruins of an antique American Republic while he recalls the poet's summary:

> "There is the moral of all human tales;
>   'Tis but the same rehearsal of the past.
> First freedom, and then glory — when that fails,
>   Wealth, vice, corruption, — barbarian at last,
> And history, with all its volumes vast,
>   Hath but one page."

THE OHIO MOUND BUILDERS.

Just what relation, geographical and ethnological, the builders of the mounds bore to the Mississippi valley and its branch basins will probably never be fully known. So far as the evidences, discovered by the early European intruder, can testify, the portion of the United States embraced within the central valley named and its tributaries, was the chief domain and center of those peculiar people, who for want of a better or more specific appellation we designate as the Mound Builders. Whether this domain was the land of his origin, a great way station in the pilgrimage of his race through its earthly existence, or was the terminus of prolonged peregrinations, has not been determined. The latest developments of science in the effort to locate the cradle of the human race, suggests, with much plausible argument, the shifting of humanity's nativity from the valley of the Euphrates to the valley of the Mississippi. Possibly science and scholarship, keen and indefatigable, may some day rend the veil and reveal the past of the earliest aboriginal Americans. Of the results of the latest investigations and the sequential conclusions of ethnology and archæology, we shall speak later on. The accumulated literature, concerning these mysterious people and their monuments, by official authorities, voluntary scientists, amateur investigators, poetic romancers and irresponsible, irrepressible and illiterate dreamers, is appalling in quantity, contradictory in statement and theory, conflicting in conclusions and often amusing and absurd. No key of knowledge has yet been found to unlock the enigma of the Mound Builder's existence. Hence the Mound Builder and his "doings" afford untrammeled scope for the imagination; he has been the subject of boundless speculation and wildest conjecture; he left literally footprints on the sands of time, but their trail leads only to oblivion; he left no written records, and his temples tell no tales as to their time or purpose; his only answer to every conceivable guess concerning his source, age and destiny is his unbroken silence; like the Sphinx of Egypt his sealed lips give back no reply, no hint, to the myriad queries as to his identity. The Mound Builder is the race with the Iron Mask; nor is there likelihood that his racial features will ever be revealed, for no oracle of learning has yet been enticed to betray his secret. The Mound Builder, whoever he was, displayed his activities in a spacious arena. No pent up Utica contracted his powers and if the whole boundless continent was not his, a large part of it was. His works extended from the sources of the Alleghany, in western New York on the east, to the Rocky Mountain range on the west, and in some instances on to the Pacific slope; the Mound Builder is almost unknown in New England; he is found in lower Canada, but evidently avoided the colder climates; in the south he was much in evidence, his works lined the shores of the Gulf of Mexico from Texas to Florida and were found in Alabama, Georgia, Louisiana, Mississippi, the Carolinas, Tennessee and Kentucky. The Northwest Territory, however, produces evidences of densest population; at least there his habitations were most numerous and important. In Wisconsin his character apparently took on a "religious turn," for along its larger river courses, he adorned the sides and summits of the hills with innumerable "effigies" of animals, birds, reptiles and human beings — presumptively tributes to his superstitious belief or symbols of his crude worship, possibly emblematic totems of his various tribes. Michigan did not greatly receive his attention; mounds occur frequently in Indiana, but are prolific in Illinois as we have noted.

Ohio was a region for which he displayed most remarkable partiality. The banks of "La Belle Riviere," as the early French called the majestic Ohio, and the pictureque and fertile valleys of the Miamis, the Scioto, the Muskingum and lesser streams were the scenes of his most numerous, most extensive and most "continuous performances." It has been asserted, without dispute, that the localities in Ohio, which testify to the Mound Builders' presence, outnumber the total localities of his evidential habitation in all the rest of the country. Ohio was the great "State" in prehistoric times, for over twelve thousand places in the present state-limits have been found and noted,

Masterpieces of the Mound Builders.

where the Mound Builder left his testimonial. These enclosures on the hill tops, the plain or river bottoms, walled-in areas, each embracing from one to three hundred acres in space, enclosures presenting a variety in design, size and method of construction, unequaled elsewhere, exceed fifteen hundred in number, while thousands of single mounds of varying circumference and height were scattered over the central and southwestern part of the state. One thing is clearly demonstrated by this tremendous "showing," viz., that these people either continued in more or less sparse numbers through a long space of time or they prevailed in vast numbers during a more or less brief, contemporaneous period, for it has been estimated that the "earthly productions" of their labor, now standing in Ohio, if placed side by side in a continuous line, would extend over three hundred miles or farther than from Lake Erie to the Ohio and that they contain at least thirty million cubic yards of earth or stone, and that it would require one thousand men, each man working three hundred days in the year and carrying one wagon load of material the required distance, a century to complete these artificial formations; or it would take three hundred thousand men one year to accomplish the same result. Supposing the laborers were exclusively men and allowing the conventional average family to each, there would have been a population far exceeding a million people. Whether these different structures were built synchronously or near the same period, we have no means of knowing. The structures were almost without exception completed before being abandoned; they left no unfinished work, from which it might be inferred that they did not depart prematurely nor in haste. Their works after their abandonment were not disturbed, except that the single mounds were occasionally utilized by the Indians for intrusive burials. The conqueror of the Mound Builder, if he had one, had respect for the spoils of conquest and left the victorious monuments inviolate and intact; pity it is the same cannot be said for his pale faced successor.

This white man's vandalism as compared with the red man's reverence for the mortuary monuments of the vanished race is interestingly expressed in the poetic lines of Mr. Thomas Backus, one of the earliest poets of the Capital City. The sentiment was suggested by the incident that a large and beautiful mound standing in the precincts of the original plat for Columbus was demolished, the clay taken therefrom and used as the material for the bricks with which the first State House was built. In this mound were found many graves filled with the crumbling bones of the unrecorded but honored dead.

> Oh Town! consecrated before
> The white man's foot e'er trod our shore,
> To battle's strife and valour's grave,
> Spare! oh spare. the buried grave.

Masterpieces of the Mound Builders. 19

> Oh, Mound; consecrated before
> The White man's foot e'er trod on shore
> To battle's strife and valour's grave,
> Spare: oh, spare, the buried brave.
>
> A thousand winters passed away,
> And yet demolished not the clay,
> Which on yon hillock held in trust
> The quiet of the warrior's dust.
>
> The Indian came and went again;
> He hunted through the lengthened plain;
> And from the mound he oft beheld
> The present silent battlefield.
>
> But did the Indian e'er presume,
> To violate that ancient tomb?
> Ah, no: he had the soldier's grace
> Which spares the soldier's resting place.
>
> It is alone for Christian hand
> To sever that sepulchral band,
> Which even to the view is spread,
> To bind the living to the dead.

It is not the purpose of this treatise to attempt any exhaustive or minute account or detailed enumeration of the vestiges left by this people. Rather is it the intention to mention, with more or less brief portrayal, the masterpieces of the different classes of their exploits. We, of course, confine our recital to the works extant in the present limits of Ohio. We will pass these works in review and discuss their origin in the following order: (1) Walled enclosures, (2)

Single mounds, (3) Village sites and burial grounds, and (4) Theories respecting the identity and existence of the Mound Builder.

The so-called "enclosures" include a great variety of structures, in which an area, of greater or less extent, is shut in. This title embraces those which cap the hill-tops and are usually regarded as "forts" or military defenses. These are built of stone or earth and in some rare instances of both. The hill-top defenses are not relatively numerous but exhibit in their construction great engineering sagacity and skill and almost inconceivable labor. The enclosures on the plains or river bottoms are almost exclusively of earthen material and are either walled towns or structures for refuge and safety; possibly some of them were religious temples. They are of all dimensions and forms, many of them presenting combinations of circles, and squares and geometrical figures of every variety. They enclose from a fraction of an acre to hundreds of acres. They are literally "wonders" and more and more excite the curiosity of the lay spectator and the awe and admiration of the archæological student.

We will look first at the "stone forts," which though comparatively few in number are of intense interest, owing to the shrewdness displayed in their location and the military instinct and engineering architecture evinced in their construction.

SPRUCE HILL FORT.

The chief of these upland bulwarks, indeed the largest stone edifice of the Mound Builders in this country, was erected on Spruce Hill, in the southern part of Ross county. This work occupies the level summit of a hill some four hundred feet in height; the elevation is a long triangular shaped spur, terminating a range of hills with which it is connected by a narrow neck or isthmus, the latter affording the really only accessible approach to the "fort," for the hillsides at all other points are remarkably steep and in places practically perpendicular. The summit commands a wide outlook over the surrounding country. Within a radius of two or three miles on the plain beneath, to the east, north and west, were groups of aboriginal works, including isolated mounds and extensive enclosures. It was the midst of a mound-building neighborhood; the site of Chillicothe, a great aboriginal center, was some eleven miles distant to the northeast. No place more advantageous for the purposes of defense or observation could have been chosen. The barrier consisted of a wall composed entirely of stone, mostly fragments of sandstone from the hill ledge and cobblestones, found in abundance on the summit. No earth was used in the wall, the line of which was carried around the hill a little below the brow. This barricade, once so complete and impregnable, is now sadly depleted and displaced; the victim of the wear and tear of hoary time, the upheaval of the elements, and the spoilation by thrifty farmers, who repair their fences with the "inestimable stones, unvalued jewels, all scattered" the summit and hillside about; most ruthless enemy of all to lay siege to the battlements were the tall primitive trees which sprang up beneath and around the curious, loose masonry, thrusting and twisting their roots among the stones and with irresistible strength lifting and scattering them apart; in many instances firmly imbedding them in their trunks; a royal battle, an irrepressible conflict, this has been between the stolid stones and the growing giants of the forest; for untold cycles, possibly for more than a millennium, this contest has been waged, and many a monarch of the woods worn and bent with the life of centuries has at last fallen in decay amid the crude and crumbling masonry, thus testifying to the vast period that this fort has stood, grim guardian of its charge. At the present time the stone structure, "trembling all precipitate down dashed," merely suggests its pristine regularity and form. The appearance of the ruins demonstrates that the line had an average base width of eight or ten feet and a height of six or eight, the stones being piled one upon the other with no other means than their own weight to hold them in place. The width and height of the wall originally varied, as the ruins indicate, according to the requirements of the summit contour and the naturally weak or strong defense features of the line followed. At the places where the approach was most easy the wall was broadest, being at points thirty feet and even more across the base. The wall is entirely wanting at one point where the perpendicular rock cliff rendered protection unneces-

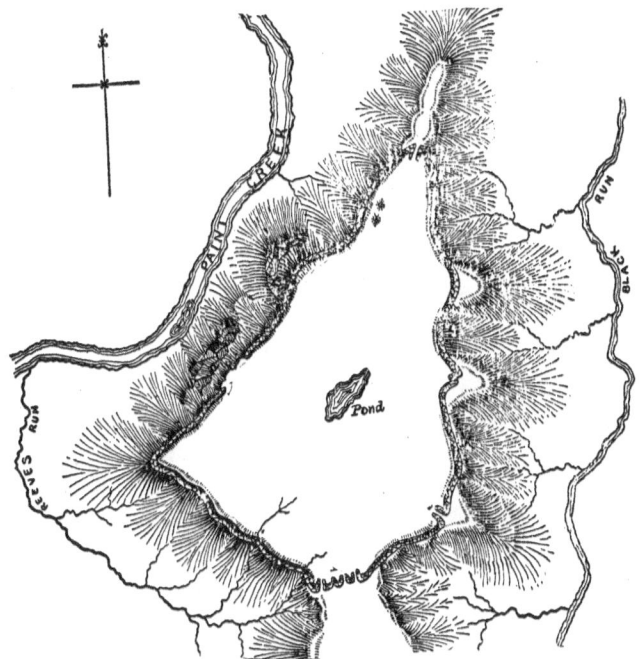

Spruce Hill Fort.

sary. Where the defense crosses the isthmus, some seven hundred feet wide, the wall was heaviest and here was the main entrance, with three gateways opening upon the terrace extending beyond. This gateway consisted of three openings in the wall, the intercepting segments of which, in each case, curving inwards, formed a horseshoe, whose inward curves were forty or fifty feet in length, leaving narrow passages, no wider than eight feet, between. At these gateways, the amount of stones is more than four times the quantity at other points of the wall, and constituted broad, mound-shaped heaps. Between these heaps, through the narrow defile, the enemy would have to pass in attempting an entrance. On the east wall apparently two other single gateways originally existed, as indicated by the curved lines, but these were subsequently closed up. At the northern apex of the fort another gateway existed, protected as the others by inward carrying walls. Excepting the isthmus, this was perhaps the most vulnerable point of the hill-top — as the sides sloped down into the valley, affording steep but possible ascent. Here the walls were unusually high and strong. The stone heaps at the great gateway give proof of having been subjected to intense heat, a feature also discernible at certain other points in the wall. Within the enclosure were found two stone mounds, located near points of the breastworks which commanded the fartherest extent of view. These mounds were burned throughout, suggesting that great fires may have been maintained thereon, perhaps for alarm signals, perhaps for religious ceremonies, perhaps for sacrificial rites.

There were several depressions in the enclosed

space, one covering two acres, which could afford constant supply of water. There was no moat or ditch at any point, either exterior or interior to the wall. The wall, continuous save at the interruptions mentioned above, measures two and a quarter miles in length and encloses an area of over one hundred and

The "Pond" in Spruce Hill Fort.

forty acres. The magnitude of this hill-top stone enclosure exceeds any similar construction attributed to the Mound Builder. It evinces tremendous labor and unusual ingenuity of arrangement. The wonder at this stupendous labor grows when it is considered that it must have been erected without the aid of beasts of burden or mechanical contrivances. It was literally built by hand labor by "piece work." Such a fortress, so situated, must have been, to a primitive people, impervious to the storm of savage warfare. It knew no surrender save to a vandal demolition of a modern, ruthless civilization; "but man would mar them with an impious hand." This effacement is of comparatively a recent date. As we learn from the investigators who first left descriptions, the result of surveys in the first third of the last century, the walls were then in a fair state of preservation and easily followed in outline and reconstructed in plan. Now obliteration almost reigns supreme. Some ten years ago, the writer with a party of experts, personally inspected the remaining ruins and from them, with slight play of the imagination, could rebuild the crude fortress. Another inspection during the preparation of this monograph, gave evidence of the final touches of a destructive hand. The line of the walls presented little more than dismantled, scattered, brush-covered heaps of grass-grown stones; the great gateway in diminished height and demolished shape was still there, as if reluctant to yield its post, grimly struggling to forbid entrance to the spacious field of growing corn that filled the enclosure; the little pond, still holding water, had shrunk to a fraction of its former size; from its depths the gutteral croak of a bull frog seemed to mockingly sound the death knell to even the memories of the greatness and glory of Spruce Hill Fort. Surely in this desolation was there theme for some poet, for an apostrophe such as Byron's on the passing of the Eternal City:

> "Come and see the cypress, hear the owl,
> And plod your way o'er broken thrones and temples,
> A world is at our feet as fragile as our clay."

Spruce Hill and Paint Creek Valley.

But there is one feature left intact. The insatiable tiller of the soil may tear down prehistoric walls to "mend his fences," and plow level the mounds erected on the plain, that he may plant a few more stalks of corn, but his greed has thus far invented no method of devastating the landscape. Nature-loving Thoreau mourned that the axe was slowly destroying his forest. "Thank God," he exclaimed, "they cannot cut down the clouds." Iconoclastic agriculture has kindly left the scene which rewards the ascent of Spruce Hill — a captivating view such as seldom

> "Hills and valleys, dales and fields,
> Woods or steepy mountain yields."

Your outlook sweeps the Paint Creek valley for miles on either side; the peacefuly flowing stream winds its way through fields glowing in the varied colors of the summer's ripening grain, all framed by the encircling, gentle-sloping, forest-clad hills. Were this scene in Bonnie Scotland, travelers would cross the sea to extol its surpassing beauty.

Fort Hill — Highland County.

HIGHLAND FORT HILL.

Much smaller though in many respects more striking than the Spruce Hill fort is the fortification in Brush Creek township, Highland county, two and a

Fort Hill (Highland Co.) — South Entrance from Outside.

half miles northwest of Sinking Springs. It is the best preserved of the stone defensive works of the Ohio Mound Builders. It was first described by Prof. John Locke, of Cincinnati, in the Ohio Geological Report for 1838. Squier and Davis made a thorough examination of it in 1846, publishing the result in their work on the "Ancient Monuments." Many surveys have been made since that time, notably one by Henry A. Shepherd, who gives an excellent description in his "Ohio Antiquities."

Fort Hill, entirely detached by Brush creek and

Fort Hill (Highland Co.) — South Entrance of Fort from Outside.

deep ravines from any other elevation, rises abruptly about five hundred feet above the river bottom. The sides for the most part present a succession of minor cliffs, shale banks, wash-outs and jutting rocks; in many places the precipitous sides shoot up in perpendicular palisades. Only at two points can the summit be reached and then by no easy effort as the writer can testify from personal experience. Encircling the top of the hill, which presents a level area of some fifty acres, is an embankment of earth and stones, mostly the latter, which were first piled up, the earth then being used as a filler, a sort of road or walk cov-

Fort Hill (Highland Co.) — Embankment, Showing General Terminus Running in from one of the Openings.

ering the top. The stone was found on the spot in the weathered fragments of the sandstone ledge which crowns the hill. The wall, which mainly follows the brow of the hill, has an average base of about thirty-five feet; its height varies from six to ten feet, though at some points it reaches a height of fifteen feet. Interior to the wall is a trench or ditch, some fifty feet in width. It was easily made by the displacement of the material for the wall. The length of this wall is between eight and nine thousand feet, or over a mile and a half. It has been estimated that it contains seventy-five thousand cubic yards of material. By glancing at the diagram it will be seen the wall-line, conforming to the shape of the hill summit, consists of four unequal sides, curved inwards and meeting in four acute points, "salient angles," at which there are peculiar open bastions, the ends of the walls running outward a little so as to protect the entrance space. The whole fort in its outline forms the figure of a "leg and foot, with slender ankle and sharp heel. the two corners of the shin and calf and the heel and the toe form the four bastions." The gateway openings are thirty-three in number and are spaces ten to fifteen feet in width, arranged without apparent order or regularity except that the same number is found on each side. The purpose of so many openings is inexplicable. They surely were not needed for ingress and egress, indeed some of them, especially the one at the northern extremity, the toe, occur upon the very steepest points of the hill, where the approach or ascent is almost impossible. This northern tip of the hill presents a bold, bluff ledge, some two hundred feet wide and rising twenty feet above the encircling wall. It is altogether the most prominent point of the hill and commands, like a sentinel tower,

Masterpieces of the Mound Builders.

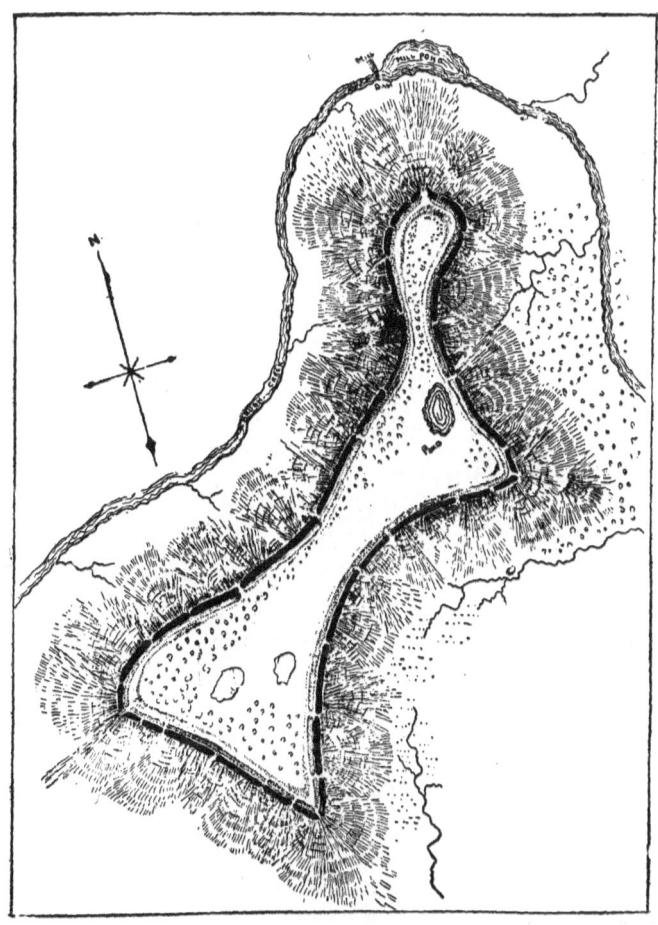

3   Highland (Co.) Fort Hill.

a wide extent of country. Here the early explorers report were strong evidences of the action of fire on the rocks. Doubtless it was the beacon station, the flaming lights of which could be seen for miles in all directions. There were within this enclosure three

Fort Hill (Highland Co.) — Embankment and Ditch, from Inside Southeast Section of Fort.

depressions or ponds, the largest of which had a well defined retaining embankment; when full the water must have covered an acre. This would indicate that this fortification was capable of sustaining a large defensive force for a long period of time. Certainly the situation and construction made it difficult to assault and well nigh impossible to capture. Its site could not have been better chosen, yet this hill was not, apparently, surrounded by any populous or numerous settlements of the Mound Builders, judging from the fact that excepting two or three isolated mounds, there is no remaining evidence of these people nearer than Serpent Mound, the most mysterious product of its creators, which was some ten miles distant. Such are the natural and artificial features of Fort Hill. The peculiar method of its construction and the inaccessibility of its location have enabled this fort to withstand the siege of time and human demolition better than the enclosure of Spruce Hill or any similar work.

It was one summer morning, just as Phoebus was starting on his daily round, that the writer and a companion, slowly ascended the steep and irregular path that leads to the southeast corner of the summit. Well rewarded were we for our perspiring pains. A magnificent stretch of golden field and green forest, sinuous stream and undulating plain, responded to our gaze. When could such a landscape tire the view? The hill, the scene, in the splendid glow of the risen sun brought to our memory its counterpart, the Wartburg hill, in the Thuringian forest, a hill similar in height and form but crowned by a ducal castle and medieval towers. Nature had given almost as picturesque a setting to Fort Hill, but here the crowning battlements were of a different age and far dissimilar architecture. We mounted the wall and pushing through the obstructing underbrush, roots, decayed trunks and branches of fallen trees, we patiently picked our way along the top of the wall for the entire circuit, the earthen filling of the embankment and the time accumulating forest-debris forming a substantial foot path.

This crude but decay-defying parapet was the cun-

Fort Hill (Highland Co.) — Showing Wall and Ditch.

ning work of the primitive savage, the ferocious warrior of a stone age; here in time of war he resorted for refuge and to light his fires to warn his people in the valley that the stealthy and relentless enemy was on the war path.

That those brave days were long, long ago, is proven by the scattered trunks and limbs of the fallen arboreal heroes and the still standing venerable giants of the forest. Every evidence of great antiquity is here presented. Hundreds of years these mammoth-trunked, lofty-limbed, old fellows had grown and wrestled with the winds and storms that beat about this fort. Some of them in hoary

Fort Hill (Highland Co.) — Embankment from Outside, Showing Steepness of Ascent.

age were to go down at last in the unequal struggle against the elements. Locke, Squier and Davis, Shepherd and subsequent experts designate chestnut and poplar and other trees still standing with the age, so they claim, of six hundred years and more. And these surviving witnesses stood over and grew from the decomposed remains, half hidden by the accumulating soil of predecessors of similar size and perhaps equal longevity. These trees, living and dead, surely turn back the hands on the dial

Fort Hill (Highland Co.) — Embankment from Outside, Southwest Section of Fort.

of time and point to a most remote period before the stone heaps were even abandoned and how long had they stood before the forest took possession is beyond human ken. What would one give for the story of this primitive fortress, its patient and painstaking builders, their life within its precincts, their feats of daring and suffering, the long starving sieges, their brave and death dealing sorties, the storm and stress of relentless conflict, when to the arrow and missels of the boldly approaching foe they returned thrusts

Fort Hill (Highland Co.) — Wall and Ditch.

of flint spears and hurlings of crushing bowlders. Could they have been recorded and preserved, may not the annals of these people have left us topics for epics as thrilling and dramatic as those of the Iliad and the Aeneid. But their heritage to us is oblivion. The only response to our earnest query for their past was the gentle flutter of the leaves as they met the morning breeze —

"Only this and nothing more."

"STONE FORT" AT GLENFORD.

A "fortification," known as the Glenford Stone Fort, is one of the most interesting and important

Fort Hill (Highland Co.) — Wall on Southwest Side of Fort. Tree Stump Estimated about 400 Years Old.

hill-top enclosures, because of its admirable location and the fact that its remains are still sufficient for its form to be easily traced and its construction to be understood. The fort receives its Glenford designation from the little station of that name, at which the tourist alights in a journey of investigation. The geography of this hill and the situation of the fort are both nearly reproductions on a smaller scale of Spruce hill and its fort. The Glenford hill, crowded by the fort, is located in the northern part of Perry county, and is the northwestern terminus of a range of upland that juts into a beautiful valley extending perhaps two miles respectively east and west. This peninsula projection is isolated from the connecting high land, except for a narrow ridge which gently declines a short distance towards the southeast, then rises to the general level. The jutting land point is elevated about three hundred feet above the Jonathan creek that skirts the western slope. The hill summit, practically level, is terminated in nearly every direction by a vertical ledge of sandstone from six to ten feet in thickness, the outcrop of the caprock. This ledge on the northwestern hill side, in many places, forms a solid natural perpendicular wall, formidable and unscalable. Indeed the hill is precipitous in its rise at all points, save at the neck and for a few hundred feet on the eastern side where the bluff is absent and the hillside, part way down, becomes a gentle slope. The selection of such a site again demonstrates the acute cunning of the Mound Builders. No locality could better answer his purpose. A hill commanding the valley; a level space for enclosure; a defense partly provided by nature and a quarry readily at hand for the masonry of his wall. Considering what must have been his mode of warfare, here could be erected a citadel that would defy attack. The wall of the fort, formed solely of the sandstone fragments found on the spot, follows closely around the summit margin except where the

Jonathan Creek Valley Looking West from Glenford Fort.

protruding ledge stratum required no artificial defense and where the hillside sloped, in which latter case the wall was continued below the summit, apparently an injudicious arrangement, though at such places the wall must have been made unusually defensive in size and form. The line of this wall, as evidenced by the remaining scattered stones, can be traced intact along its entire length, though so many of the stones have been hauled away it is difficult to determine the original dimensions and shape. The total length was 6,610 feet, something over a mile and a quarter, and it is safe to conjecture that while hav-

Glenford Fort — West Wall.

ing a varying size, as the sections of the summit to be protected required, it must have had an average of ten or twelve feet in base and a general height of six or eight. At the southeast corner was the chief gateway opening upon the isthmus connecting with the extending hill range. Here the wall was reentrant along the sides and greatly strengthened, as at Spruce Hill. We have said this was the main gateway, indeed it may have been the only one, as there is now no positive evidence of any other. There was

Glenford Fort — East Wall.

no moat adjoining the wall. The area enclosed was about twenty-six acres and is clear of all stones, presumably all having been gathered up to form the walls — except those used to construct a large stone mound, located as indicated in the diagram. This mound was conical shaped, one hundred feet in diameter and within the memory of persons now living was some twenty feet high. It has been greatly disturbed by explorers. The purpose of this mound can only be guessed. Possibly it was the look-out or signal station. A smaller stone heap formerly existed in another part of the fort. On several of the hills flanking the Jonathan creek valley were earthen mounds the fires of which could easily have been seen from this fort. Indeed the gentleman, a resident of Glenford village, who acted as our guide over the fort, informed us that extending across the country for a distance of some twenty-five miles was a series of hill-top mounds, so placed that smoke or fire signals could be exchanged between them. On one hill some two miles west of the fort was an earthen wall enclosure encircling two or three acres, presumably a defensive work. Evidently in Mound Building days there were great "doings" in these parts and as our aforesaid guide remarked, "those old fellows, whoever they were, knew their business."

This fort was early made famous by Caleb Atwater, Ohio's first historian and archæologist; he was a graduate of Williams College; a lawyer, member of Ohio Legislature and Indian commissioner under Andrew Jackson. He was born on Christmas, 1778, in North Adams, Massachusetts. In 1815 he made Circleville (Ohio) his home and there resided till his death in 1867. He was a man of great scholarly attainments, a prolific and forceful writer. He made extensive study of the works of the Ohio Mound Builders. He visited the fort — afterwards called Glenford — in 1818 and carefully describes it in an elaborate report he made to the American Antiquarian Society of Worcester, Mass. This report was published in the proceedings of the Society for 1820. It is interesting and instructive to recall what such an authority said at so early date concerning this fort. Mr. Atwater writes:

"This large stone work contains within its walls forty acres and upwards. The walls, as they are called in popular language, consist of rude fragments of rocks, without any marks of any iron tool upon them. These stones lie in the utmost disorder, and if laid up in a regular wall, would make one seven feet or seven feet six inches in height, and from four to six feet in thickness. I do not believe this ever to have been a military work, either of defense or offense; but if a military work, it must have been a temporary camp. From the circumstance of this work's containing two stone tumuli, such as were used in ancient times, as altars and as monuments, for the purpose of perpetuating the memory of some great era, or important event in the history of those who raised them, I should rather suspect this to have been a sacred enclosure or 'high place,' which was resorted to on some great anniversary. It is on high ground, and destitute of water, and of course, could not have been a place of habitation for any length of time. It might have been the place, where some solemn feast was annually held by the tribe by which it was formed. The place has become a forest, and the soil is too poor to have ever been cultivated by a people who invariably chose to dwell on a fertile spot. These monuments of ancient manners, how simple and yet how sublime. Their authors were rude, and unacquainted with the use of letters, yet they raised monuments, calculated almost for endless duration, and speaking a language as expressive as the most studied inscriptions of latter times upon brass and marble. These monuments,

Masterpieces of the Mound Builders. 47

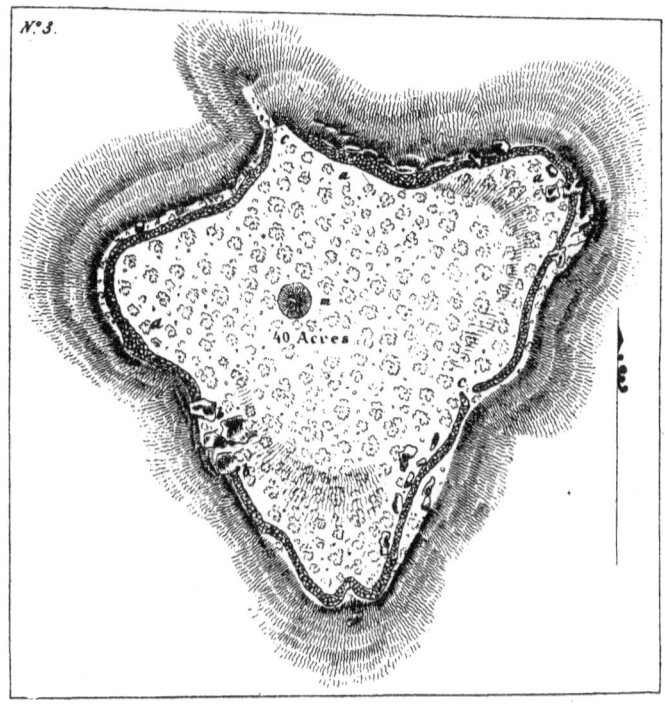

Glenford Stone Fort — Perry County. Design of Col. Whittlesey in Smithsonian Contributions to Knowledge. (1850.)

48   *Masterpieces of the Mound Builders.*

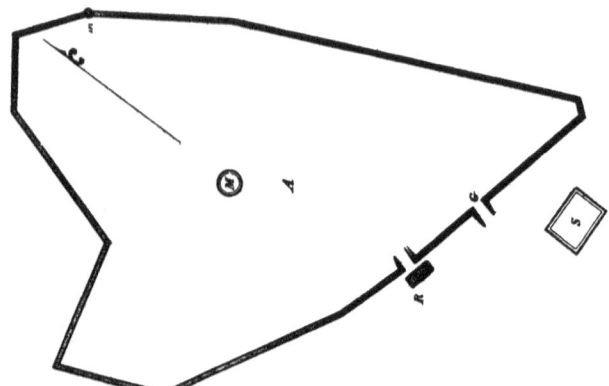

Glenford Fort from Plan Made by Caleb Atwater 1818 and Printed in Proceedings American Antiquarian Society 1820.

their stated anniversaries and traditionary accounts, were their means of perpetuating the recollection of important transactions. Their authors are gone; their monuments remain; but the events, which they were intended to keep in the memory, are lost in oblivion."

So appeared this fort ninety years ago. To-day Stone Fort is a most attractive place to visit, the view from the hill top presenting the little valley and encircling miniature mountains, is a scene to please the eye and stir the poetic sentiment. The old fort is a romantic ruin, for mingled with its scattered and crumbling crude masonry are the trees of all ages, growths, shapes and varieties; maple, oak, beech, chestnut, elm, poplar, ash and others canopy with overhanging branches the moss grown stones of the walls and with their clutching roots push the sandstone blocks asunder. In one striking instance a sturdy century-old poplar had entwined his roots about the wall and pried them beneath the surface layer of the bed rock; the storm came and overthrew the tree; the firm grasp of its underground branches lifted the natural stone foundations upright, creating

Glenford Fort — West Wall.

a perpendicular wall some ten feet square, level as a marble floor and encased in a lace net work of roots and tendrils, as the leaden filigree interlocks the glass figures of cathedral window:

"Who can impress the forest, bid the tree unfix his earth-bound root?"

50   *Masterpieces of the Mound Builders.*

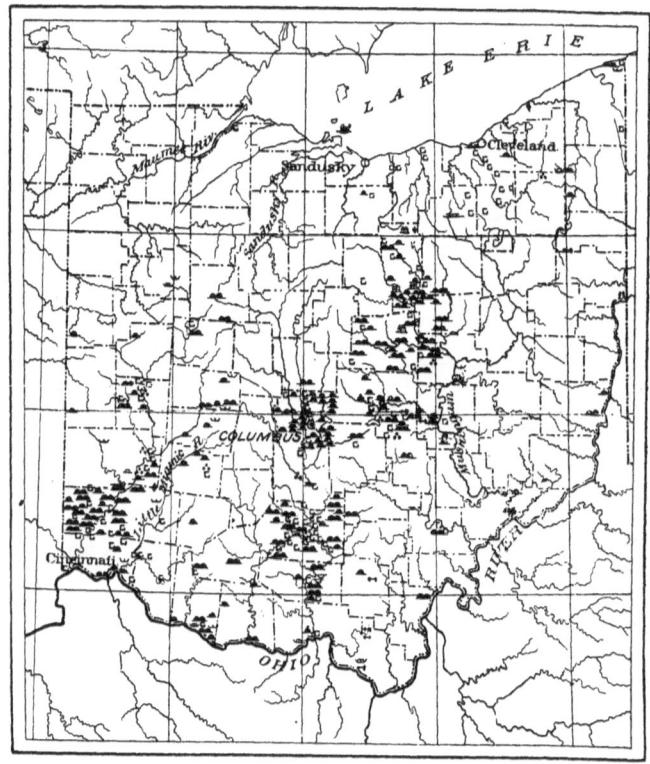

Archæological Map of Ohio — Showing Chief Mounds and Enclosures of Prehistoric People. From the reports of the Smithsonian Institution by Cyrus Thomas, in 1891.

Masterpieces of the Mound Builders. 51

At Glenford Fort the pranks of nature were scarcely less interesting than the proofs of the prowess of primitive man.

MIAMI FORT.

By glancing at the archæological map of Ohio, it will be seen that the southwest portion of the state, especially the valleys of the Great and Little Miamis,

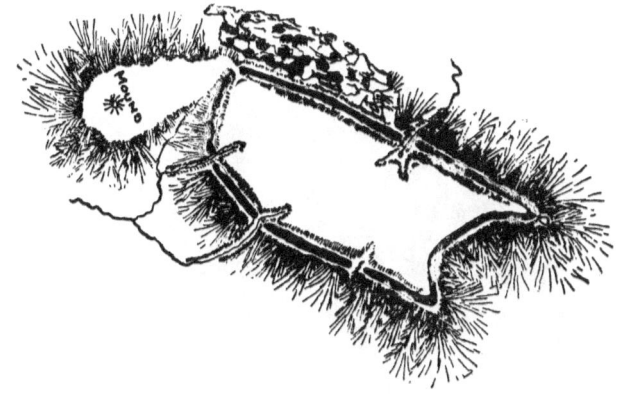

Miami Fort.

was the region most crowded with the habitations and monuments of the Mound Builders.

Within the present limits of Hamilton county, between four and five hundred mounds and some fifteen important enclosures were noted by the early travelers and settlers. The most famous and noticeable of the latter is the one on the "Fort Hill at the mouth of the Great Miami." It has been generally

52   *Masterpieces of the Mound Builders.*

designated as the "Miami Fort," but this Miami fort must not be confounded with the historic Fort Miami, the first fortification in Ohio, built first by the French in 1680 and rebuilt by the British in 1785, at the foot of the rapids of the Maumee.

The "Miami Fort" is small in size but important

Walls and Gateway — Miami Fort.

in situation and suggestion. It was first brought into notice in the literature concerning the Mound Builders by William Henry Harrison, who though a Virginian by birth became an Ohioan by adoption, marrying a daughter of John Cleves Symmes and settling at North Bend, where his remains are now buried. General Harrison was a man of unusual literary and historical acquirements, and had he never been known as a general or president he would have won distinction as a scholar. He profoundly studied the Ohio Mound Builders and the Ohio Indians and we are indebted to him for much valuable investigations and information on those subjects. He carefully surveyed "Miami Fort," giving his results in a scholarly address, published (1839) in the Transactions of the Historical and Philosophical Society of Ohio. We give his plan as adopted and reproduced by Squier and Davis. The site of this fort is strikingly analogous to the hill forts heretofore described. The Great Miami, flowing southwest, debouches into the Ohio at a sharp angle. An upland elevation, some two hundred feet or more in height, thrusts its nose prominently out into this land angle, separating the two rivers. On the peak of this elevation is the fortification. It is very nearly a parallelogram in shape, conforming to the summit contour of the hill. The walls are unusually massive and strong, the mean cross-section being considerably in excess of that of any other enclosure in the state. These ramparts, in places sadly depleted, are in large measure well preserved and though

> Here giant weeds a passage scare allow

and sections of the protective works have been

> Swept into wrecks anon by Time's ungentle tide;

the experienced explorer may easily follow the lines of defense, which are from thirty to fifty feet at the base with a height of ten feet or more. They are built of earth and stone, the latter being plentifully used to give strength and stability to the earth filling.

Section of Wall — Miami Fort.

Three or four gullies have worked their way into the fort, but the gateways or artificial openings could not have been more than two or three in number. The declivities on the north and south sides of the fort are precipitious and in the olden days must have been almost unascendable, indeed for some distance

Masterpieces of the Mound Builders.   55

on either of the longer sides, so perpendicular are the hillsides that it is quite impossible to detect the line dividing the hilltop from the base of the wall. The area enclosed is only about twelve acres. It was a snug little fort. Below the southwest wall, facing the Ohio, is a gentle slope, leading to the summit of

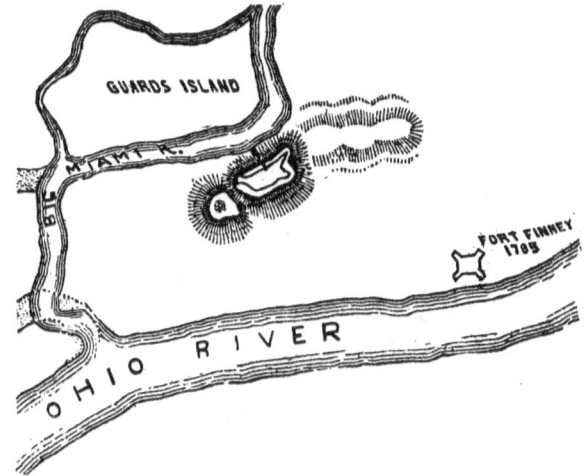

Miami Fort — From Indiana Geological Report for 1879.

a "nub" or circular spur of the hill, upon which is a conspicuous mound, some fifty feet in diameter and originally, probably, ten to fifteen feet in height. It has been much plowed down. From this "observatory" mound one obtains the most entrancing view in the state of Ohio. The valley of the Great Miami is at your feet on the west; just across the gently flowing stream are the hilly ranges of Indiana, through which courses the White Water River, mingling its singularly pure blue and green water with the muddy yellow of the Miami, just a mile or two above the latter's entrance into the Ohio. On the south at your feet with majestic swerve sweeps the

> "Ohio-peh-li! Peek-han-ni! The pride
> Of the land where thy waters, O-pel-e-chen, glide;
>
> * * *
>
> Through thy vales, and the hills in the distance that loom,
> Seen far through the azure, or lost in the gloom,
> Have long been the homes of the noble and brave,
> Whose proud halls are built on the Indian's grave."

Stretching along the south banks of the Ohio are the rolling hills of "Old Kentuck," the sunny land of "Dixie." The rushing waters of these uniting rivers bring to the mind a flood of historic memories, in the days of discovery and frontier settlement. Down this Ohio and up this Miami came the chivalrous and grotesque expedition of Celoron from Quebec with his Indians in feathers and war paint and his French soldiers in the gay trappings of a medieval crusade. At the mouth of La Riviere a la Roche, as the French then called the Great Miami, Celoron moored his little navy of birch bark canoes and with courtly and dramatic ceremonies planted his last lead plate, proclaiming that these rivers and all their tributaries belonged to his majesty, Louis, King of France. That was August, 1749. And then the little white fleet of twenty or more light gondolas pushed up the "a la Roche" to Pickawillany, carrying the Bourbon banner across the Buckeye State.

But before all this, centuries and centuries before, this beautiful scene of hill, vale and river had a geologic record. It was a mid-summer day, that Pro-

Junction of Big Miami and Ohio River — From Miami Fort.

fessor G. Frederick Wright and the writer, stood on the summit of that outlook mound, and reveled in the riches of the charming landscape, the scene being softened to an artistic atmosphere by the hazy, fleecy clouds through which the rays of the August sun were tempered. My distinguished companion told the story of the creation of this panorama; how it took millions of years to mold this land and carve out the great heights and depressions and then how the final touches were put to the picture by the icy fingers of the glacial hand; how the great frozen avalanche came down the trough of the Ohio and meeting an obstruction near this point, choked the channel and formed a glacial dam high enough to raise the level of the water five hundred and fifty feet, forming the "Ohio Lake." The glaciers acted as great freight cars and hauled down sand and gravel and covered the hillsides and filled the valleys. The mouth of the Great Miami was the southwest point of this great ice bed in Ohio. That was decades of centuries before the Mound Builders climbed the steep hill, erected their stronghold and, according to General Harrison, made their last stand for their Ohio land. The general claimed to have discovered evidences of a defensive line from the base of the hill on one side to the Ohio and on the other side to the Miami — enclosing a bottom plain of three hundred acres. This was to preclude a flank attack on the fort. He surmises the Mound Builders may have been the **Aztecs**, and says if they were really the Aztecs, "the direct course of their journey to Mexico and the facilities which that mode of retreat would afford, seem to point out the descent of the Ohio, as the line of that retreat. It was here (Miami Fort) that a feeble band was collected to make a last effort for the country of their birth, the ashes of their ancestors and the altars of their gods."

Commanding the rivers as it did, Miami Fort was certainly one of the most strategic points of the Mound Builders' system of defenses. Several archæ-

Section of Wall — Miami Fort.

ological authorities, particularly General M. C. Force, whom we cite, in his valuable essay on the Ohio Mound Builders, point out that from this elevation (Miami Fort) a line of signals could be put in operation, which in extent would cover the southwestern portion of the state:

"Three great works on the Great Miami, one at its mouth, one at Colerain, and one at Hamilton, with subsidiary defensive works extending six miles along the river at Hamilton; several advanced works to north and west of Hamilton, on streams flowing into the Great Miami; and other similar defenses farther up the river at Dayton and Piqua, all put in communication with each other by signal mounds erected at conspicuous points, constitute together a connected line of defenses along the Miami river; Fort Ancient on the Little Miami stands as a citadel in the rear of the center of this line. A mound at Norwood, back of Cincinnati, commands a view through a depression of the hills at Redbank eastwardly to a mound in the valley of the Little Miami; northwardly through the valley of the Millcreek and the depression in the land thence to Hamilton, with the works at Hamilton; and by a series of mounds (two of which in Cincinnati and its suburbs have been removed) westwardly to the Fort at the mouth of the Great Miami. So a series of signal mounds along the Scioto from the northern boundary of Franklin county to the Ohio river, a distance of over one hundred miles, could transmit by signals an alarm from the little work north of Worthington through the entire length of the valley to the works at Portsmouth."

Less extensive systems of stations in this wireless telegraphy have been clearly established in other sections of the state, such, for example, the one mentioned in connection with the Glenford Fort. One of the prominent hills in Indiana which was within signaling range of Miami Fort, was crowned with a prehistoric fortification, thus establishing interstate (?) communications.

BUTLER COUNTY FORT.

In prehistoric times, no less than later in the pioneer days, the Great Miami must have been a great water way, for along its valley plains were numerous sites where dwelt the Mound Builders, while many

View of Big Miami Valley from Fortified Hill — Butler County.

of the hill-tops, on either side, were capped with walled enclosures or various shaped single mounds of these ingenious and mysterious people. After entering the river on his northern voyage to Pickawillany and the portage from that river to the St. Marys, Celoron passed beneath the war-like embattlements of many an earthen fortification. These dirt-built "strongholds" defended the hill summits, no less securely than the stone turrets guarded, like grim sentinels, the rocky cliffs of the romantic Rhine. Doubtless these simple, crude bulwarks of clay on the heights of the Big Miami were in place before the

View of Valley from Fortified Hill — Butler County.

German Barons erected their towered castles. After paddling past four or five of these ancient fortresses, deserted and tenantless then as now, the plucky sailors of the little French fleet might have sighted the shadows of a peculiarly protected muniment which we call the Butler County Fort, because located in that county, three miles below the present town of

Masterpieces of the Mound Builders. 63

Hamilton, and some thirty miles from the mouth of the Great Miami. The valley at the point in question is imposing in width. The hill, the summit of which the fort occupies, is on the west side of the river, perhaps half a mile distant from its present channel, and rises to an elevation of two hundred and fifty feet, a height considerably above any other in the vicinity. The section of the state now comprised in the county named was thickly strewn with the works of these ancient people, several hundred of their mounds and enclosures being in existence when the early travelers first had their attention called to them.

This fort had a special significance, both in its well chosen location and the peculiar features of its design. It was accurately described by Mr. Squier in a concise pamphlet, published in New York in 1847. He made a careful survey of the works, the plat of which was afterwards used in the extensive volume of Squier and Davis.

This fort hill, like nearly all of the heights similarly protected, is the termination of an upland range that extends out like a long tongue into the valley. It is surrounded at all points, except the narrow neck towards the north, by deep ravines, presenting steep and almost inaccessible declivities. The slope towards the north is very gradual and from that direction the hill crown is easy of approach. Skirting the brow of the hill and generally conforming to its rim, was the artificial wall of earth and stone, having an average heighth of five feet with a base of thirty-five.

64　*Masterpieces of the Mound Builders.*

Those were the dimensions as the parapet stood when viewed by Mr. Squier. The earth composing the wall was a stiff clay having for the most part been taken up from the hill surface, without leaving any perceptible excavation. The length of the wall embankments was about three-quarters of a mile not counting the

Largest Portion of Wall on Fortified Hill, Three Miles south of Hamilton, Butler County.

gateway defenses, and the area enclosed was some seventeen acres. The hill summit, thus enwalled, rises gently on all sides from the rim towards the center, forming a knoll or camel-hump which at its greatest altitude is some twenty-five feet above the encircling walls. From this apex one may overlook not only the

Masterpieces of the Mound Builders. 65

fort side but the entire surrounding country, presenting the Great Miami valley on the east and the Valley or Indian Creek on the west. This scene is an encore of the miniature mountainous ones we have beheld from the previously described fortified hills. We are obliged to rely mainly upon the earlier report of Mr. Squier for the detailed accounts of this interesting fort, for it is now sadly ruined, indeed for the most part practically obliterated, for these defenses, which in their prime were impervious to the attacks of a savage foe, armed with flint pointed spears and stone battle axes, have fallen an easy prey to the invincible steel of the plow share. On our visit we found the fading lines of the earthen walls overgrown with forest trees and almost obscured by impenetrable underbrush and tanglewood. Faint outlines remain of the famous north gateway and its crescent outpost. For it was the complicated protection to the four gateways or openings, three at the southern extremity and one at the north, facing the land neck, that peculiarly classifies this fortification. The accompanying diagram will best designate their position and form. Interior to the openings were "covering" walls of a "most singular and intricate description," a series of overlapping labyrinthian breastworks, so fashioned that the entering enemy would become entrapped between them. This scheme at the north gate is especially elaborate, while exterior to the gateway was a massive crescent-shaped mound extending across the land neck, convexing towards the plateau that afforded the approach to the fort. This gateway plan is in almost exact correspondence to the so-called Tlascalan gateways, em-

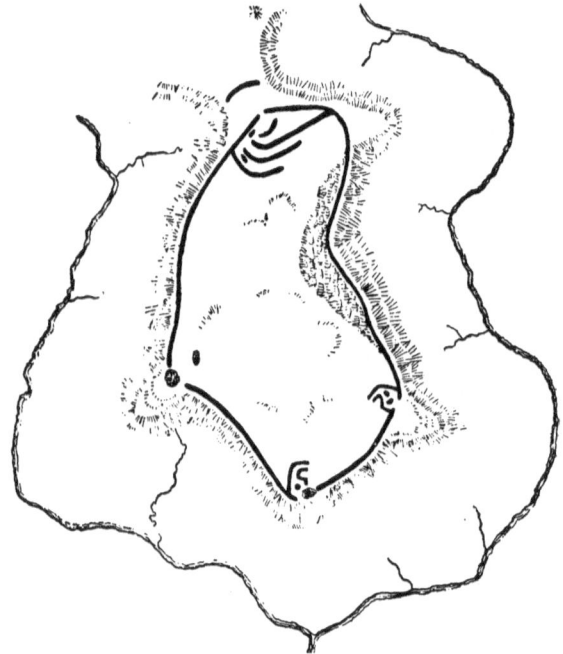

Butler (County) Fort — Three Miles below Hamilton.

ployed in the stone wall defenses of the province of Tlascala, Mexico, and described by Cortez and other early Spanish writers. This form of gateway, with variations, is found in other works of the Mississippi and Ohio valley Mound Builders and leads to the inference that there was some ethnical relationship between the Ohio Mound Builders and the ancient Aztecs and Toltecs. Interior to the northern wall

Interior of Fort, Butler County, Three Miles South of Hamilton, Author Standing in Remains of One of the Dug-holes."

there is still evidence of a ditch, while at various points within the enclosure there were "dug-holes," from which it appeared a portion of the material was obtained for the walls. Some of these pits are yet clearly definable, indeed still "hold water," being doubtless originally used as reservoirs.

Three or four hundred feet north of the fort on the level isthmus are the remains of a conical mound, thirty feet in diameter and now some ten feet high, surmounted by several trees of venerable and stately growth. It is recorded that years ago, the mound was partially excavated, the only result being the discovery of a quantity of stone which had been subjected to the action of fire.

As our party approached the mound we were greeted by a couple of bareheaded, barefooted country boys who with youthful curiosity and energy had dug into the base of the tumulus and exhumed a skeleton, the bones of which lay heaped before the uncovered grave. The skull upon exposure had parted into fragments, the teeth falling into the cranium cavity. It was a comico-serio incident, the grewsomeness of it being no little enhanced by the moisture-sodden atmosphere that hung like a clammy cloak about us beneath the heavy threatening sunless clouds. The settings of the scene were cheerless, but the boys gleefully poked with their muddy feet the disinterred human relics, clay-stained and decay-eaten;

"In nature's happiest mould however cast,
To this complexion thou must come at last."

"For even Imperious Cæsar dead and turned to clay,
Might stop a hole to keep the wind away."

Had this disjointed frame been that of a great war chief, "the hero of a hundred battles," or perchance a "silver-tongued orator" rousing with his eloquence his fellows to deeds of valor, in whose honor his sur-

Mound North of Butler Fort.

viving tribesmen had erected this earthen monument? There could be no answer to our guesses, but there came to our mind, as we gazed upon the bones denuded of their earthy covering, the poem of Bryant on the "Disinterred Warrior.:"

Gather him to his grave again,
    And solemnly and softly lay,
Beneath the verdure of the plain,
    The warrior's scattered bones away.
Pay the deep reverence, taught of old,
    The homage of man's heart to death;
Nor dare to trifle with the mould
    Once hallowed by the Almighty's breath.

The soul hath quickened every part —
    That remnant of a martial brow,
Those ribs that held the mighty heart,
    That strong arm — strong no longer now.
Spare them, each mouldering relic spare,
    Of God's own image; let them rest,
Till not a trace shall speak of where
    The awful likeness was impressed.

For he was fresher from the hand
    That formed of earth the human face,
And to the elements did stand
    In nearer kindred than our race.
In many a flood to madness tossed,
    In many a storm has been his path;
He hid him not from heat or frost,
    But met them, and defied their wrath.

Then they were kind — the forests here,
    Rivers, and stiller waters, paid
A tribute to the net and spear
    Of the red ruler of the shade.
Fruits on the woodland branches lay,
    Roots in the shaded soil below;
The stars looked forth to teach his way;
    The still earth warned him of the foe.

Masterpieces of the Mound Builders. 71

A noble race! but they are gone,
  With their old forests wide and deep,
And we have built our homes upon
  Fields where their generations sleep.
Their fountains slake our thirst at noon,
  Upon their fields our harvest waves,
Our lovers woo beneath their moon —
  Then let us spare, at least, their graves.

Sample of skeleton found in Ohio Mounds. This grave opened in Baum Village Site.

FORT ANCIENT.

The chief masterpiece of the Mound Builders is known as Fort Ancient. For imposing grandeur in size, ingenuity in design and perfection in construction it is easily the first among the prehistoric fortifications and is regarded as representing the highest point attained in earthwork structures by this lost race. When one has visited St. Peter's Cathedral he has witnessed the sum total of ecclesiastical architecture and when one has stood within Fort Ancient he has seen the most majestic monument erected by the people who were its constructors. All honor to the State of Ohio, its possessor, and the Ohio State Archæological and Historical Society, its custodian, that this priceless and unique work is today in excellent state of restoration and preservation. An ac-

Entrance to Fort from West, Looking East.

count of this work, accompanied by a correct plan, which we herewith reproduce, appeared in the "Port Folio," a magazine published in Philadelphia for the year 1809. The author of this initial treatise on the subject, with modesty conspicuously rare in early researchers, omitted his name. The plan and description were copied by Mr. Atwater in his report to the American Antiquarian Society (1820) and republished in his "Western Antiquities," printed in Columbus (Ohio), 1833. It was also briefly described by Dr. Daniel Drake, in a chapter on antiquities in his "Pictures of Cincinnati," published in 1815. The fort was also carefully studied and mapped "from a faithful survey" by Prof. John Locke of Cincinnati, the map and description being published by him in 1843 in the papers of the American Association of Geologists and Naturalists. This map, which we also herewith reproduce, and Locke's description were incorporated in the work on the "Ancient Monuments of the Mississippi Valley," by Squier and Davis, published by the United States government as the first volume of The Smithsonian Contributions to Knowledge, printed in 1848. Squier and Davis supplemented Locke's description with one of their own. These diagrams and descriptions were the substantial bases for subsequent students and surveyors. Judge L. M. Hosea, of Cincinnati, made a personal study of the works in 1874, giving his conclusions in a scholarly article published in the "Cincinnati Quarterly Journal of Science" for October of that year. The learned editor of the American Antiquarian (Chicago), Dr. **Stephen D. Peet, has written many articles upon** this inexhaustible theme. The most distinguished archæologists of the country have made it a study. Professors J. W. Powell, Cyrus Thomas, Frederick W. Putnam, W. H. Holmes, G. Frederick Wright, John T. Short, M. C. Read, Gerard Fowke, General M. F. Force, Colonel Charles Whittlesey, Mr. Henry A. Shepherd and many others of equal or less distinction have contributed by their studies and writings to the literature concerning this famous chef d'æuvre of the ancients. Models of it have been made for many of the museums of Europe and famous savants from all parts of the world have journeyed to America to verify the accounts sent broadcast concerning it. The proverbial Britisher who failed to find anything worthy of notice in this new country — because it was so "deucedly devoid of ruins, dontcher know," should have had his attention called to Fort Ancient. His longing for antiquity would have been supplied. He should have asked for what he did not see. It would have been forthcoming.

In August, 1898, the annual convention of the American Association for the Advancement of Science was held in Columbus. On the last day of the session a special train, under the auspices of the Ohio State Archæological and Historical Society, carried the delegates of the Archæological and Ethnological Section of the Association to Fort Ancient. A luncheon

Masterpieces of the Mound Builders. 75

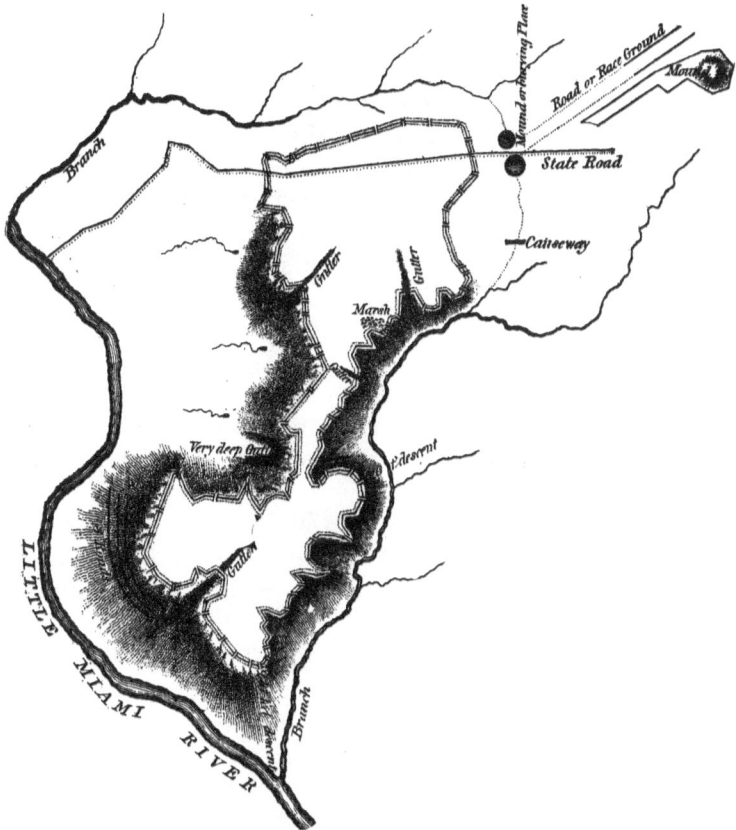

Plan of Fort Ancient Published with an Explanation in the Portfolio (Philadelphia) for June, 1809. First Illustration of Fort Ancient Ever Made. Reproduced from the Original.

was served to over a hundred guests gathered about the table spread within the great gateway of the Old Fort. After dinner speeches were made by several of the most distinguished archæologists of the country. All paid high tribute to the wonderful works of a vanished race and to the enterprise of the Ohio Society for securing and preserving this greatest of all their monuments. In the fall of 1902 the International Congress of Americanists, the leading students of archæology, from all parts of the world, met in New York City. They desired to see Cahokia Mound and Fort Ancient; on their way to the former they spent a day at the latter, the guest of The Ohio State Archæological and Historical Society. There were in the party the official national representatives of the Archæological Departments of Canada, Mexico, Argentine Republic, Costa Rica, Uruguay, France, Germany, England, Sweden and Russia. The visitors were greatly delighted and astonished in their examination of the extensive fortifications of the people of a lost empire. Even the youthful and practical United States could produce prehistoric remains of surpassing magnitude and symmetrical proportions, outdoing similar exhibits in the older countries. They all acknowledged it was the most wonderful specimen of its kind, probably in the world.

The latest and most detailed investigation of the fort was made by Professor Warren K. Moorehead, who first visited it in 1885 and whose subsequent explorations covered in the aggregate more

Masterpieces of the Mound Builders. 77

than forty- three weeks, scattered through the years 1888, 1889, 1890 and 1891. The results of his researches are incorporated in his two interesting works entitled, respectively, "Fort Ancient" and "Primitive Man in Ohio." He was assisted in the work by Mr. Gerard Fowke, author of the Archæological History of Ohio, published by the Ohio State Archæological and Historical Society, and Mr. Clinton Cowen, official surveyor for Hamilton county. The two latter gentlemen made a careful survey of the works and drew the map which is now the accepted authoritative outline of the fortification.

LOCATION OF THE FORT.

The site selected by its builders for this greatest fortress, grandest temple or largest walled city, which ever it may have been, was most advantageously chosen, on a slightly rolling plateau, overlooking the valley of the Little Miami River, in central Warren county, some forty miles northeast of the mouth of that river, where it enters the Ohio at Cincinnati. The river at the point in question, coming from the north, flows through a most picturesque valley perhaps a mile in width and flanked on each side by elevated uplands. On the east side a section of the elevation is nearly separated from the adjoining plateau by two deep ravines, beginning within a few hundred feet of each other, the one, starting north and then running west, enters the Miami valley, the other starting south curves to the west, debauching into the same valley. The plat, accompanying this description and made especially for this publication, shows these ravines and their creeks. This plateau is about three hundred feet above the river level. The banks of these ravines form steep sides on the east

Entrance to Fort from the West.

and on the north of the peninsula which they cut off; the only approachable way to the peninsula being the neck or strip of level plateau between the heads or sources of the two ravines. The west or Miami side of the hill is for the most part abrupt and difficult of ascent. The ravines on the east, north and south

Masterpieces of the Mound Builders. 79

of the hill are exceedingly irregular in outline, creating sharp curves, jagged points and irregular indentations in the hillside, at one point, near the center of the hill, these ravines almost unite, leaving a narrow neck only about five hundred feet wide. Here the declivity on each side is very steep. Around this peninsula, on the very verge of the skirting ravines, was built the wall of defense; meandering around the spurs, recoiling to pass the heads of the gullies, it is so zigzag in its course that its entire length is 18,712 feet or more than three and one-half miles, while the direct line from the north wall to the south wall is only 5,000 feet or less than one mile. Something over one hundred acres, Moorehead says one hundred and twenty-six, are enclosed within the walls. This enclosure is divided by the contour of the embankments into what are known as the North or New Fort, the Middle Fort and the South or Old Fort. The terms "new" and "old" were suggested by the idea that the south fort would naturally be the first one to be constructed as it, utilized alone, would be more secure and inaccessible than the new — which latter was "later" taken in to protect the entire hilltop. This supposition, like much that is put forth concerning the fort, is however a fanciful guess.

The traveler alights from the train at "Fort Ancient Station," a collection of hotel, store, postoffice and three or four houses, by no means the "loveliest village of the plain," yet so lapsed into "innocuous desuetude" that compared to it, Goldsmith's famous "deserted village" was a scene of exciting activity. In the seasons of the year when the trees and hillsides are stripped of their foliage, from the station one can plainly see the walls which cap the hilltop. A circuituous and strenuous climb of nearly a mile up the Lebanon and Chillicothe Pike brings one to the main entrance, marked "A" in our outline diagram. The impression is at once created that one is entering an imposing structure of some kind; these gateway walls on either side are massive in base and height, rising with hump back summits above the continuing walls which they terminate. This gateway has probably been widened by the pike. As one passes through, a view is obtained of a long stretch of lofty and shapely walls on the east side of the New Fort. This sight is at once reassuring — the visitor is now certain there is to be no disappointment about this "famous fort;" it is not the fiction of imagination, you are really going to see all and more than you expected; your interest and wonder are at once aroused, Fort Ancient, whatever its origin or purpose, it itself no myth.

The wall deserves careful study. It is a marvelous piece of defensive construction. Its width, height and contents vary as the requirements of the hill top and the proposed formidableness of the defense demands. The base breadth is from thirty to fifty feet, in some places as much as seventy, the height from ten to twenty-two feet, measuring from

Masterpieces of the Mound Builders. 81

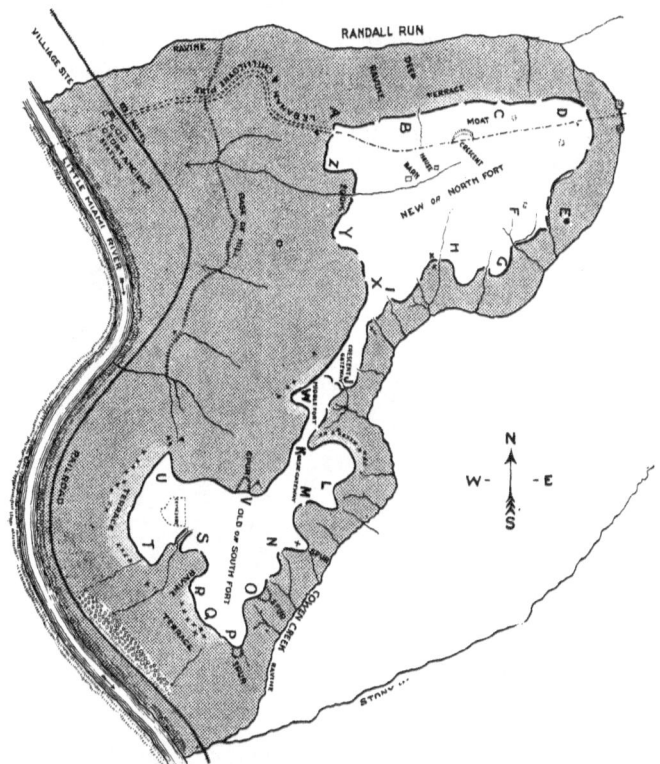

Diagram of Fort Ancient, Designating Points as Described in the Text.

the level of the fort interior. The wall's surface has an outward slope from thirty-five to forty-three degrees. This wall height is much increased at places on the interior by a moat or ditch from which the material was taken to build the barricade. This moat at places was found to be originally from two to seven feet deep, but has at all points been greatly

Entrance to Fort from Inside Looking West.

filled in by the natural slow deposit of decayed accumulation, leaves, wood, vegetable matter, soil, etc. At some sections of the wall, particularly in the new fort, where the wall on the east faces the open plateau a moat was built exterior to the wall. Whether these inside "moats" were built as such or were merely the incidental depressions created by the removal of the earth for the wall is a disputed point.

It has been suggested that these moats, or some of them, where especially wide and deep, may have been utilized as reservoirs or artificial ponds in which to store water. The soil from which the embankment is built is a tough, diluvial clay or loam. This consistency of the material has been an important factor in the preservation of these walls.

At the risk of tedium and monotony, let us circumambulate these walls. It is a journey as entertaining as it is exhilarating, occupying three or four hours — the only means of obtaining a true appreciation of the extent and ingenuity of this unequaled enclosure. The walking for the most part is good; the wall top is everywhere so spacious and level that were it not for the innumerable trees that pre-empt the way and the breaks made by the gateways and gullies, one could drive a "coach and four" along the summit.

THE NORTH WALL.

We climb the wall on the left, the western point of the north wall of the New Fort. This wall extends almost due east and west for a distance of nearly half a mile. It follows along the summit edge of a deep ravine which at its western outlet almost deserves the title of valley. The base of this ravine is the bed of a little stream designated as Randall's Run. The south side of this ravine which the walls face is very steep, the ascent being quite impossible. This wall, strong and well preserved, varies in height and width and is broken by some nine or ten openings, natural or artificial. In several places gullies, which cut into the steep sides of the ravine, extend up to and through the fort walls. These natural openings, the gullies or cuts made by the outflow of water from within the fort and those made by the gradual approach or ascent of the gullies from the valley ravines below can be accounted for. The artificial openings or gateways, over seventy in number in the entire fort, are not so easily explained as the number of them is far in excess of the apparent necessity for purposes of egress and ingress and moreover they are frequently at places where the ascent or descent of the hillside is now practically impossible. We will discuss these gully openings and gateway passages later on. The north wall from "A" to "B" is especially well formed; through this three gullies have cut their course, the most westerly one in a particularly distinctive way. Below the wall from "B" to "C," some thirty feet down the declivity, the steep hillside is checked and presents a "terrace" or level landing, perhaps a thousand feet long and one hundred broad. These hillside terraces occur at many other places in the hillsides leading up to the fort. They are the subject of much discussion, the query being whether they are natural or were made by the Mound Builders. Our answer would be probably in most instances "natural," possibly in rare instances artificial, not unlikely they might in some places be both at the same time, the original formation being employed to complete a "platform." These terraces in

Masterpieces of the Mound Builders. 85

many places were used as burying grounds as we shall see; to what other use they may have been put is a matter of conjecture. This terrace, we first see, has every appearance of being simply a natural shelf in the hill. Fort Ancient is so extraordinary itself that

Entrance — Fort Ancient Park, North Fort.

it creates the tendency on the part of many students and spectators to give an unusual interpretation to every accessory feature. This tendency has led to many most fantastic conclusions and grotesque statements. About opposite the center of this **north wall,** and curving into the present roadway, is a crescent-shaped mound, originally two hundred and seventy feet in length, its convex side facing the wall. It is now but few feet high, having been badly defaced. Returning to the wall, it is noticed that at points, particularly from "C" to "D," it has been carried below the summit level, the fort interior rising above it. This occurs at only a few other places in the construction of the fort. Within the north wall, especially along the eastern end, is a moat, or ditch, formed by the

Section of East Wall, North Fort.

removal of the soil for the wall. In this moat much water now stands, indeed has been of so long standing that a willow tree has risen from its flag and rush-filled pool to add its weeping presence to the great variety of other trees that stand like rows of sentinels on the fort walls; a long file of stately soldiers they make; beech, ash, hickory, elm, walnut, cherry, poplar, sugar, oak, gum, buckeye, occasionally a silvery sycamore, stand guard along the parapets which they well nigh have made immovable and

Masterpieces of the Mound Builders. 87

imperishable, their tough embracing roots, like bands of iron and hoops of steel, grasping the earth erections and holding them firmly in place. The north wall at its east end where it turns toward the south is carried to an unusual height, for here the gorge has tapered to a narrow wedge; the wall leaves the steep ravine side and the level plateau begins, affording a point the enemy might well select for a stealthy assault from the ravine head. At "D" is the gateway, at the northeast corner of the enclosure.

PARALLEL WALLS AND PAVEMENT.

Before continuing our walk we go outside a few hundred feet east on the pike to see the two mounds, one on each side of the road from which began the Parallel Walls. These mounds originally ten feet high and forty feet in diameter are some sixty feet apart. On being opened they were found to contain nothing but some charcoal flakes and a few pieces of broken pottery. From each mound extending east there was built a low earthen roadway elevation, a foot or more in height, twelve feet wide, and a little more than one-quarter of a mile in length. At the eastern end these elevations came together in a circular curve, within the center of which curve was a little mound. These earthen parallel lines are now entirely obliterated but were clearly traced by earlier investigators and were defined and described by Prof. Moorehead. What they were for "nobody knows." A reasonable presumption would be that they were in some way connected with the games, possibly ceremonies of the builders. Similar structures have been found in other places in Ohio. They have been more often than otherwise dubbed "race courses." It may have been a gauntlet ground. Between these parallel walls, extending from the west end, for more than two h u n d r e d feet was unearthed a "stone pavement." It was first discovered, about 1868, by Mr. George Ridge who resided on the north side of the pike a short distance east of the north m o u n d. This "pavement" lay from one to three feet under the present soil surface, and was built of limestone s l a b s, averaging a b o u t a foot in length, six inches in width and two and a half inches in thickness. Its width was the space between the parallel walls, averaging seventy-five feet; its length appears not to have been definitely determined, the statements, by different authorities, concerning the same, varying from one hundred to five hundred feet. It lay, of course, beneath the present pike. In places the stones

Entrance to Fort from East, Looking West. On Each Side of this Road Ran the Parallel Walls.

Masterpieces of the Mound Builders. 89

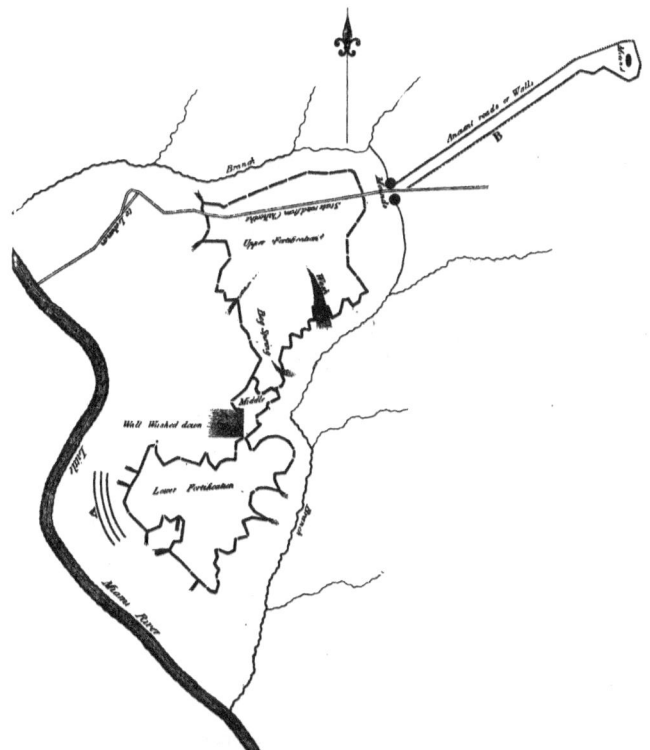

Fort Ancient. Plan by Caleb Atwater in American Antiquarian Society Proceedings, 1820.

showed evidences of having been subjected to great heat and all were somewhat worn on the upper side or surface, not by "the inaudible and noiseless foot of time," but, so the discoverers claim, by the feet that trod incessantly to and fro or by those that "tripped the light fantastic," as more than one writer thinks this was a place of amusement, a sort of assembly hall for aboriginal gaiety. Perhaps the first published notice of this "pavement" occurs in *The Cincinnati Quarterly Journal of Science* for July 1874. That number gives an account of a visit to Fort Ancient by The Cincinnati Society of Natural History, the party consisting of some fifty gentlemen, scientifically and archæologically inclined. In the report of that excursion occurs the following:

> "It is said that a pavement of thin limestone has been discovered a foot or more below the surface of the ground, and extending several hundred yards in a southeast direction from these mounds, and I saw in the field nearby many of these flat stones that had been plowed up, and upon digging a foot or more in depth at this place found the pavement, and lifted up some of the thin, badly weather-worn stone, which had evidently been placed where found, because the diluvial soil and drift was several feet thick below them. The excavation and work at this place was under the direction of Mr. Hosea and J. Kelly O'Neil, who were fully satisfied that they were lifting up the pavement laid by the subjects of the king of the Mound Builders anywhere from ten to five hundred thousand years ago, as it best suits the imagination, always being willing to rise or fall a peg or two to suit the taste of the inquisitor."

Judge L. M. Hosea in a subsequent number of the *Journal of Science* (1874) gives at length a most

Masterpieces of the Mound Builders. 91

interesting and scholarly description of the Fort. In relating his investigations of the pavement he indulges in a pleasing fancy over the scene suggested by the stone floor and its accompanying parallel walls.

"Imagination was not slow to conjecture up the scene which was once doubtless familiar to the dwellers at Fort Ancient. A train of worshipers, led by priests clad in their sacred robes, and

Roadway Approaching Entrance to Middle Fort.

bearing aloft the holy utensils, pass in the early morning, ere yet the mists have risen in the valley below, along the gently swelling ridge on which the ancient roadway lies. They near the mound, and a solemn stillness succeeds their chanting songs; the priests ascend the hill of sacrifice and prepare the sacred fire. Now the first beams of the rising sun shoot up athwart the ruddy sky, gilding the topmost bough of the trees. The holy flame is kindled, a curling wreath of smoke arises to greet the coming god; the tremulous hush which was upon all nature breaks into vocal joy, and songs of gladness burst from the throats of the waiting multitude as the glorious luminary arises in majesty and beams upon his adoring people. A promise of renewed life and happiness. Vain promise, since even his rays can not penetrate the utter darkness which for ages has settled over his people."

Professor Moorehead thinks this stone platform was for the purpose of a dry floor, when the surrounding ground might be wet and muddy, upon which the natives could hold dances, while the mounds and parallel walls "would afford an excellent position for on-lookers and for squaws who would beat tom-toms and accompany the dance with their usual doleful singing." He adds: "We believe this is the only instance of ancient pavement proven beyond a doubt in the Mississippi Valley * * * the earth, which accumulated over them (stones) would give them an age of several hundred years at least." He designates the date of their placement at 1400 A. D., but acknowledges this is "conjectural."

If this "floor" really existed to the extent claimed, its purpose will doubtless have many more guesses coming. As certainly may this "arrangement" have been the scene of religious incantations, sacrificial rites, a "den of superstition," perhaps the burning-stake-field for the captives, the apostates, the traitors, and the condemned criminals.

EAST WALL.

But we turn from "this pleasant place of all festivity," or "chamber of horrors," whichever it may have been, to resume our discursion along the walls. The stretch of defense in four divisions from "D," the eastern gateway, to "E" is the most clear cut and "fortlike" perhaps in the enclosure. These walls

East Wall (North) Fort Ancient from Field Outside

defend the interior from the level field that like a great plain sweeps to the east toward Chillicothe. These walls loom up straight and shapely and cut the horizon like pyramids in the desert. The first three of these sections are separately, 85, 110 and 159 feet in length, they are some seventy feet broad at the base and twenty-three feet high. They are among the noblest examples of Mound Builders' defensive battlements. It is outside these walls that the wide and deep moat existed. Water stood therein continuously until a very recent date. This ditch must have been an intentional moat to protect the walls which here defend the most exposed approach to the fort. The moat inside is shallow, at least now; it must have been filled in by the work

East Wall, North Fort.

of time. The open gateways, ten feet or less across at the base, are perfectly preserved. Why the openings in the most vulnerable point of the fort? Much speculation has been indulged thereat. In many of the enclosures in the valleys or river bottoms, elsewhere in the state, these openings are protected by conical mounds immediately before and within the open space; in some fortifications this mound is convex or horseshoe shaped, as the stone one on Spruce Hill and most notably at Miami Fort. Not

Masterpieces of the Mound Builders. 95

so at Fort Ancient. The artificial gateways gape wide open and give no hint of protective features. It has been surmised that originally these breaks were built across with palisades or stockades or that fence-like wooden shields were set back some distance before the passage space like a great screen before an open door. Many insist that even on the walls themselves a palisade fence was built. But the evidence of such in the way of decayed wood, post holes, etc., is wanting, not only at Fort Ancient but in the mound structures elsewhere. The Mound Builders in their mounds and defenses seem to have adhered strictly to earth or stone material, except in their graves and burial chambers. Dr. Selden S. Scoville, in an address (1892) before the American Association for the Advancement of Science, suggests these gateways may have served as places where the besieged could make sallies and retreats, in order to decoy the enemy within the enclosure to be captured. For we know that almost all barbarous people regard the capture of their enemies as of more importance than killing them in battle. Mr. Thomas J. Brown, editor of the *Miami Gazette* and a devoted student of Fort Ancient, which he began to visit fifty years ago, has the following theory concerning the gateways:

"In reading descriptions of Fort Ancient we notice constant allusion to its numerous 'gateways,' and these are generally coupled with expression of wonder that there should be so many. Now I have made these 'gateways' my special study during my whole acquaintance with it. I have walked the whole length of the ramparts and counted every footstep and every gap, and carefully noted the distance of these gaps apart, and long ago concluded that there are but about five bona-fide gateways, the rest being intended rather for points of defense than for places of ingress and egress. The earthen ramparts would afford little protection to the defenders in case an assault were made upon them. The inside slopes are as steep as the outside and afford no suitable standpoint, so the defenders' bodies would be protected and yet give him an opportunity to see over the rampart. If he stood upon the top he would be even a better target for the assailants than they would be for him. I consider it necessary to conclude that each of these gaps was occupied with a blockhouse reaching out beyond the wall, forming a bastion from which defenders could enfilade the outside of the ramparts most effectually. The distance of these gaps apart is in no case too great to serve this purpose, and if we consider it in this way, the whole outside of the walls could be defended with very little exposure on the part of the defenders. There was evidently one gateway where the public road now enters from each side, and one at the extreme farthest end of the 'old fort,' one near the middle of the north side, and one most likely on the west side opening from the peninsula, and one nearly opposite on the east side. The rest of these gaps were intended merely to give opportunity for introducing blockhouses at proper distances and in proper positions for defense, and may have been supplied with small wickets, easily closed and easily defended. Even the acknowledged gateways were probably built in the same general way, but with the portal idea unmistakable and prominent."

From "E" to the incising gully "F" is a deep moat. The ravine of Cowen Creek here begins to carve down the hillside; the channel of this creek grows deeper and steeper as it plows its way south till, at the southeast corner of the fort-hill, it unites

Masterpieces of the Mound Builders. 97

with Stony Hollow Creek, which latter flows from the northeast and empties into the Miami. These ravines, with their radiating gullies, make the hill summit exceedingly irregular and jagged. The walls follow the crest-line closely; in order to do so they make many a sharp turn and often a quick reversal. Indeed the wall is largely a row of horseshoes or convex curves between the intervening gullies. The moat

Section of East Wall (South) Fort Ancient from Inside.

interior to the eastern and southern walls of the New Fort, "F" to "I," is very marked. From the gully "F" to gully "H," there are several artificial openings in the wall and some of them at places where the ravine side is so precipitous that a gateway would be superfluous, if not absolutely useless. Some of these "openings," however, offer peculiar construction. The moat, in these cases, stops at the base of the opening or is filled in, leaving the interior surface continuous through the gateway, and in not a few instances, outside the walls before the opening, is built a little platform, a continuation of the level walk which passes through the opening. These walkways, through and beyond the gateways, are very

Entrance to Middle Fort or Crescent Gateway Looking South.

distinct in places. This exterior "platform" might be used as a lookout or sentinel stand, and especially would this landing be of advantage when located on the edge of an inaccessible declivity. These external platforms occur most frequently along the east wall of the fort, suggesting the idea that attack was most

Masterpieces of the Mound Builders. 99

feared on that side, yet the west side of the fort which was more approachable, has fewer of these platform projections.

GREAT GATEWAY.

At "I" the hilltop narrows and the isthmus or neck begins. The neck at this point is not over two

Great Gateway from the North.

hundred feet wide and advances with varying breadth for a quarter of a mile, nowhere exceeding three hundred feet in width and terminating at the narrowest point less than one hundred feet across, at the entrance of the Old Fort called the Great Gateway. The walls on either side of the isthmus are the lowest and least formidable of any section because the natural protection on each side of the isthmus is the greatest. Near the center of this isthmus where it widens to two hundred and fifty feet the erecters of the fort built the Crescent Gateway; a sort of intermediate barricade. It consists of two curving mounds, side by side, each convexing toward the north and extending to the walls on either side of the neck. This seems to mean that the enemy would be expected to first attack the New Fort and if successful then advance along the neck and assault the Old Fort. The Crescent duly manned would check if not defeat the enemy's progress. This Crescent Mound is entirely and adroitly in accord with the whole scheme of the fort defense. The space between the Crescent and Great Gateway is called the Middle Fort. On both sides of this section the hillsides are unusually steep and rugged, being cut by deep gorges, the walls are therefore lower than elsewhere and for a short distance entirely lacking; the perpendicularity of the hillside being sufficient protection against approach. The Great Gateway is flanked on both sides by walls that are strengthened and enlarged; heaps of stones being used in their erection. Indeed the walls which here curve in to make the narrow passage, allowing no more room than would permit a wagon to pass, look from either side more like separate mounds than sections of the continuing wall. The passage path between these mounds is elevated, so as to give an incline inside and out, thus adding to the facility with which ingress could be prevented. This citadel of the fort is the acme of the engineering plan; it is literally the *piece de resistance* that awakens admiration for the military genius of the Mound Builders. Here science weakens before sentiment and poetry

The Great Gateway from the North.

gets the better of archæology, for just inside the Old Fort on the west, as you emerge from the Great Gateway, is a conical mound, ten feet high, with a base diameter of forty feet, near which were found heaps of stones, used both as coverings for graves and to strengthen the wall. Human bones in vast quantities — "bushels of them" — were found here a few inches below the surface soil. Was this the burial spot and was this mound the monument to heroes who, battling bravely for the "pass," like the three hundred of Grecian glory, sank never to rise again,

> The hopeless warriors of a willing doom,
> In bleak Thermopylae's sepulchral strait.

What bloody encounters here occurred, how this narrow passage was piled with the bodies of the dead and dying we can never know, for

> Here, where they died, their buried records lie,
> Silent they speak from out the shadowy past.

OLD FORT.

We are now inside the Old Fort. From the Great Gateway the two walls which constitute the Old Fort greatly diverge, one runs directly east, the other southwest. The wall on the left from the Great Gateway, as you enter the South Fort, makes a lengthy curve toward the east, conforming to the hill contour ("K" to "L"). This wall carries a wide and deep interior moat; exterior to it, thirty or forty feet down the steep incline, is a terrace, narrow, shelving and long. This terrace is located in the wildest portion of Fort Ancient. The ravine here is deeper than ever, the side below the terrace nearly perpendicular; on this terrace were innumerable burials, the graves being of the crudest sort, the interments very shallow, and covered with plentiful supply of stones. It was surely a fitting spot for the undisturbed repose of the warrior. Under the very walls in whose defense they may have sacrificed their lives; on the brink of a wild, foreboding ravine, so indicative in its nature of their own savage lives, the babbling brook and soughing tree-branches sang the requiem

Mound in Old Fort Just Inside Great Gateway.

of the buried. Was ever a more secluded bivouac for the dead? But if curse was uttered against any who might move those bones, it phased not the archæologist, for as one walks along the wall that looks down upon this barbarian cemetery one may see the desecrated tenantless sepulchres and the scattered stones, the pitiless work of curious scientists.

Between the "L" and "M" angle is a gateway opening out upon a spur platform such as has been previously mentioned. The trench within the wall is most marked. From "N" to "O" the cliff is unusually steep and the wall less defensive. At "O" is one of the most extensive spur tables in all the range of the walls. From this point in the absence of foliage the eye could follow the full length of the Old Fort east wall. The southeast corner of the Old Fort ("P") offers another spur commanding a most splendid view of the Stony Hollow ravine as it extends from its narrow source to its broad entrance into the Miami valley, on the right. This is a scene of wildest tiny grandeur, if one may so speak, for the spectator stands far above the lofty tops of the trees which fill and pack the ravine and crowd up its straggling broken hillsides. It is a little black forest; the interlocking branches of the elbow-touching trees shut out the struggling sunbeams and the shadows cast their gloom over the open spaces of

"The sunken glen, whose sunless shrubs must weep."

It must have been such a compact, dense army of tree-tops that appeared to the frenzied imagination of Macbeth when told that "Birnam wood do move to Dunsinane."

Betwixt the platform gateway at "Q" and the angle "R" the wall has a wide moat within, while beneath the wall outside is another terrace, not very distinctly formed, but serving as another cemetery, for here numerous graves were found. The gully marked "S," midway in the hillside and wall of the Old Fort, is exceedingly broad and cavernous, the breach in the earth works being a hundred and fifty feet or more in extent. The hill brow was originally carved out by a broad curve, as in-

Section of South Wall, Old Fort.

dicated by the wall following the edge, but the gully subsequently cut under and through the wall, making the ugly scission noted. We mention this as a sample "wash out" which the archæologists and geologists utilize as an age indicator. The theory and claim is that in the cases where the gully or ravine has destroyed the wall and invaded the fort interior, the time which nature required to extend the ravine to its present limits within the walls, measures the age of those walls. These geological timekeepers tell us some of these ravines were many hundreds of years in working themselves out, even five and six thousand years are among the figures mentioned in connection with this fort.

But has nature always run her ravine trains according to unchangeable geologic time tables? Without attempting the scientific diagnosis, this in substance is the method of notation, and it is given without comment for what it is worth. It is certainly more reasonable than some other methods of so-called scientific computation.

In some instances the apex or head of the gully where it clipped the hilltop would be walled across, the wall instead of going around to avoid the cut and shut it out, would be depressed down the near side, across the bottom and up the other side without a break. This was doubtless the case in some instances where now the wall is gone, the gully subsequently carrying away the transversing embankment. Again in places, as may be seen, the gully was filled with the base of the wall, the summit level of the wall presenting no irregularity or depression.

From "T" to "U" are three long stretches of strong walls. The entire length faces a terrace, too ill-defined and too natural appearing to claim artificiality, at least to the eye of the layman. Along this ledge

Masterpieces of the Mound Builders. 107

were found burials and it is to be noted that these terrace graves are almost confined to the hillsides of the Old Fort, a few being discovered on the slight spurs beneath the west wall of the isthmus. Whether the existence of these burials in connection with the South Fort strengthens the claim of a greater age for it than for the North Fort, we do not assume to say.

THE CEMETERY.

In the center of the Old Fort was located the cemetery, the largest burying ground of the fort people. Within a radius of a hundred feet, in all directions, some three hundred graves were found and over a thousand wagon loads of stones were removed therefrom by different excavators. Professor Moorehead found twenty skeletons. The graves were sunk an average depth of two and one-half feet, and were formed of limestones which were plentiful in the ravines and river bottom below. The stones were arranged around the sides, head and feet and over the remains of the interred bodies. We reproduce, by permission, an illustration from Mr. Moorehead's work, of one of these interments, the covering layer of stones, of course, being removed so as to expose the skeleton. Buried with it were a large spear-head of yellow flint, remains of broken pottery and a large stone celt, a chisel or axe. The skeletons were in various stages of decomposition and generally crumbled to dust on being exposed. The space between the encircling stones and the body was usually filled in with earth. The graves in this cemetery were almost uniform in construction. These skeletons showed little or no difference in size and form from the modern conventional skeleton. The "skulls were well shaped,"

Stone Grave and Skeleton as Found by Prof. Moorehead in the Cemetery of the Old Fort.

and Professor Moorehead thinks, presented two types of mentality, a lower and a higher order. He further claims that the tree growths surmounting some of these graves indicated that the burials antedated the period when the Indians were known to have first immigrated into or occupied this portion of the country; i. e., the post-Columbian historic tribes, such as the Delawares, Shawnees, etc. Mr. Warren Cowen for the past ten years the custodian of the Fort, states that he removed from the space including the cemetery the stump of a walnut tree which a distinguished botanist estimated to be between four and five hundred years old. The conclusion however, that the fort antedates the Indian invasion is questioned by some archæologists and ethnologists. When doctors disagree, who shall decide? The reader pays his money — for this book — and takes his choice. There can be no absolute decision.

The graves on the terraces were in the main similar in construction and contents to those found in the interior of the cemetery. In many cases the stones were more plentifully employed. Some of the terrace graves contained a combined number of burials; a sort of group tomb. One "tomb," located on the ledge west of the Old Fort and overlooking the Miami valley, which Prof. Moorehead mentions, contained in its makeup a quantity of stones equal to one hundred wagon loads; when found they were lying in a layer two feet thick and spread over a space twenty feet wide — the width of the terrace — and fifty feet long. It required the labor of three men for two days to displace the loose masonry of this crude mausoleum. Fragments of twenty skeletons were exhumed from this plural grave. The skulls were crushed, the jaws broken, the body bones wasted and scattered, but such leg and arm pieces as were found entire testified by their size and shape that the deceased were people about the same stature as the present Americans, though "with greater strength and powers of endurance." If there were giants in those days, as some ethnologists would have us believe, they were not in evidence at Fort Ancient, so far as the "exhibits" prove. Many children were buried on the terraces.

GRAND VIEW POINT.

But we turn from these sepulchral features of the fort to "take a more cheerful view." This is obtained from the sharp angle of the wall at "U." We call it Grand View Point. A smart spur of the hill juts out over the valley depths. The spectator is on the highest eminence of the hill and looks north upon an amphitheatre; a circle of hills rise on all sides and enclose the valley and river of the Miami;

"Rock, river, forest, mountain, all abound."

Whether the Mound Builder was consciously or unconsciously touched with the spell of pleasing scenery, he invariably choose, in his upland habitations, locations that offered the most attractive display of natural beauty. This lookout sweeps a vista that one is loth to leave; the historic Little Miami here passes through the most picturesque setting of its entire course; the forest clad hills gently slope to the grain clothed fields, through which the river gracefully winds. From this vantage place, too, can be seen the full mile length of the western wall, crowning with its undulating height and deviating curvings the zigzag summit of the hill, the steep side of which is slashed with gullies and streaked with the

Little Miami Valley Looking North from Grandview Point.

gravel and alluvial deposits of a glacial period, for ages or eons ago, the geologists say, this peaceful and verdure adorned valley was a lake, upon which colossal cakes of ice floated and bumped against each other. Many of these ice floats were driven by the winds or shoved in the 'push" upon the hillsides and there dumped their loads of sand and debris. This western hillside was once well covered with the glacial floatage. The ravines came later, tearing away the gravel covering and digging into the clay and limestone of the hill. Thus there were great geological "goings on" in these parts before the Mound Builders came upon the scene of action. We could not qualify as an expert on this subject, but we offer the probability that the so-called "terraces" above mentioned were not hand-made by the Mound Builders but rather were the handiwork of the geological activities, long "before the war" of the Mound Builders. We are upheld in this position by the fact that similar platforms are found on the hill slopes of the opposite, western side, of the valley, where the Mound Builder left no evidences of his habitation or presence. Professor Moorehead, however, insists that these terraces, or at least some of them, are artificial; that they were built by men and used as burial sites and vantage ground in war. He says "The claim that these were made by glacial action and have no work of man about them, cannot be substantiated. It is not possible that water could deposit so regular a line for so long a distance. Moreover, these terraces are not gravel; they are limestone clay; and their formation could not result from glacial action."

STONES IN WALL.

But we resume our trudging along the wall top. We follow the "battlements," swerving in and out, descending the end of each separate section, springing across the opening, and up again on the opposite

West Wall, North Fort near Entrance to Middle Fort.

side of the gateway, here and there coming abruptly face to face with a washout or gully; some of these we descend to clamber up the corresponding acclivity; occasionally a wall gap is "too fierce to tackle" and we go around and resume the wall at its continuation. This wall, by the way, is composed almost entirely of the soil from the fort interior, as before stated. Stones however are used, often at the gateway ends, to better secure their retention of form; again where the wall is unusually large or the descent on the outside especially precipitous, stones are used as "steadiers" or strength and form retainers. Portions of the west wall on the isthmus are said to be composed almost entirely of stone. In two or three places, for a short distance, stones were laid on the wall top as a sort of walk. In some places Professor Moorehead found layers of stone through the center of the wall as revealed by the transverse cutting of the gully. At one point the wall seemed to have been built in two horizontal sections with time intervening; built half way up, covered with a layer of stones and then left till it was grown over with grass and small sprouts and covered with vegetable matter. Upon this beginning a subsequent layer of earth and stones was placed to complete the wall. But the fortifications seem in the main to have been erected by one continuous labor. Stones were seldom used ex-

Ravine Back of Custodian's House.

cept at the gateway ends and where the wall might need especial strengthening as the toughness of the soil composing the wall gave it sufficient self-sustaining trength and permanency.

Passing north along the west wall of the isthmus we re-enter the New Fort, the southern and western wall of which is badly broken by wide

West Wall (North) Fort Ancient.

and impassable gullies, the main one of which, like an immense crack in the hill, extends almost to the center of the Fort. The opening where the walls cease on either side is two hundred feet or more across. How much of this cavity was cut before the fort was reared, is hard to tell. This is one of the gullies the geologist might wrestle with in his time calculations. If it antedated the ancient fortifiers, it would seem natural for them to have carried the wall along the sides of the gap to estop ingress from the gully. The wall-ends on each side appear artificial, i. e., they appear to terminate as originally intended for they unquestionably continue down the gully side gradually tapering off till lost in the ravine bank; possibly there was little or no intervening break when the wall was built and that a whole section of the defense was gradually eaten away. We do not know. All other vulnerable points on the hill were so carefully and laboriously guarded, the apparent neglect of this break baffles explanation. Passing around this gully we soon terminate our circumambulation of the walls; we have completed the great circuit; we finish at the pike gateway, where we entered. It has been a strenuous tramp but the result is amply compensatory, for in no other way can one get an adequate idea of the extent and ingenuity of the fort, the natural advantage of the hill, and the scenic attractions its location presents.

THEORIES CONCERNING THE FORT.

We have seen and studied this vast monument of the Mound Builders, the greatest architectural product of their labor and genius now extant. What does it all mean? Its age and purpose have elicited every variety of conjecture. For we can only conjecture. We cannot know. Taking into account the different evidences of its antiquity — geological, ethnological and archæological — it is safe to say it

Masterpieces of the Mound Builders. 117

was completed and abandoned at least five hundred years ago, or a century before Columbus discovered this continent. It most likely was in existence five hundred years before that, or a millenium before now. This would carry us back to the heart of the Dark Ages in European events; antedating the Norman Conquest of the Anglo-Saxons; to the time of Alfred the Great, before the conquering Canute ordered back the waves of the sea; before Macbeth murdered Duncan and before the Crusaders began their pilgrimages to the Holy Sepulchre.

Who the people were to whom the builders of this fort undoubtedly belonged we will discuss later on. We say this "fort," because every reliable evidence and reasonable inference leads to that conclusion. In this nearly all the better and safer scholars agree. As sustaining the "fort theory" we quote from the article in *Science* (1886) by Prof. Cyrus Thomas, certainly one of the highest authorities on the prehistoric works in America, he says, speaking of Fort Ancient:

"That it was built and intended as a work of defense, is so apparent that it is scarcely possible there should be conflicting opinions on this point. The situation chosen, and the character of the work, seem sufficient to put this conclusion beyond all doubt. Yet there are few, if any, satisfactory indications, aside from the character and extent of the work, that any portion of the inclosed areas was occupied for any considerable length of time as a village site. That a work of such magnitude and extent could have been hastily cast up for temporary protection, by a savage, or even a semi-civilized people, is incredible. Moreover, there are reasons for believing that the whole fort was not built at one period of time, but was progressive. The southern part was apparently built first, the northern section being a subsequent addition, made possibly because of increase in the population, most likely by the incoming parties or clans seeking protection."

It would be entertaining to recite all the curious purposes attributed to this work. One thinks it was a great relief map of the continent of North and South America, the lines of the new and old forts making a striking resemblance to the outline of the Western Hemisphere. Another that the walls of the two forts resemble two great serpents turning and twisting in a deadly conflict — as the serpent was the chief symbol of those primitive people. Another regarded it an immense trap to secure game. The hunters would form lengthy lines the country around and drive the buffalo, deer and wild game into this corral, where the animals could be retained and killed at pleasure — a sort of commercial slaughter house or aboriginal meat trust! Others concluded it was a vast holy temple, in which religious ceremonies of great and imposing nature were at times celebrated. Again it is merely a walled town, but mostly it has been designated, as before stated, a military fortress, the safe retreat and refuge for the population of the surrounding country. To our mind it is not improbable that it was the fortified capital of these people in the Ohio valley. May it not have been the national fortified seat of government, the federal headquarters of the confederated tribes?

Masterpieces of the Mound Builders. 119

Certainly it was the center of a great Mound Builder population. The Miami valley in this neighborhood was alive with these people, as the various scientific explorations indubitably testify. At the base of the fort hill, on the broad bottom of the river, was a village site great in extent; one mile and a half below the southern extremity of Fort Ancient was "another large village covering some eight or ten acres, rich in graves and debris. Two miles up the river is still a third, so large that it must have been occupied by two or three hundred lodges — while at the mouth of Caesar Creek, six miles to the north, are two extensive sites, one in the bottom and the other upon the hill to the south." All these were carefully explored under the direction of Professor F. W. Putnam, of the Peabody Institute. These sites and others abound in the immediate vicinity of the Fort, while the whole southwestern part of the state is an area thickly covered with the remains of this extinct race, as a glance at the archæological map by Professor Cyrus Thomas will reveal.

FORT VILLAGE.

That the fort itself was to a certain extent, at least, a walled city, is proven by the remains of a "village" explored by Professor Moorehead. This village was in the Old Fort and adjacent to the cemetery already described. The evidences were the "circles" of burned earth, ash heaps, pottery and animal fragments, bear, deer bones, charcoal, burnt stones, etc., marking the places where "wigwams" or lodges had been erected. In short the same discoveries that disclose village sites elsewhere. No metal implements of any kind were found, unless it be a few small pieces of native beaten copper. These lodge circles were from 22 to 30 feet in diameter the soil of the area enclosed being of a different color from the earth outside. These lodge floors, when uncovered, were found several inches beneath the accumulating surface soil. In the moats and ditches buried beneath the later filling were found similar debris, suggesting that these habitations occasionally occupied the inner edge of the ditch and that "refuse was thrown into it just as our housewives would throw rubbish from the kitchen into a lake, river or pond" adjacent to the house. Thousands of primitive implements used in war, the chase and domestic life, arrow and spearheads, axes, skinning stones, etc., were found in the fort precincts, indicating great active life therein. Outside the

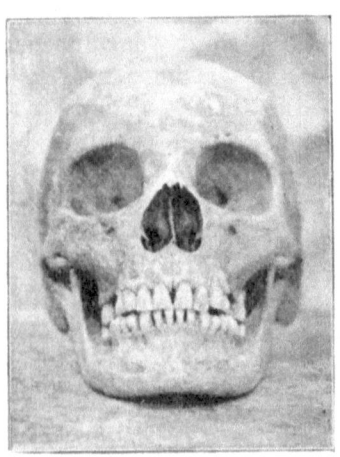

Skull of Woman Found by Prof. Moorehead in Stone Grave in the Village Site.

Masterpieces of the Mound Builders. 121

northeast gateway of the New Fort, a short distance away, on the farm of Mr. Ridge were found in the area of about an acre vast quantities of flint clippings, consisting of countless pieces of unwraught flakes and innumerable fragments in various stages of workmanship, of arrow and spear heads, knives, awls, needles, etc. This field of flint must have been the storehouse or "factory" where implements used in peace and war were made. Professor Moorehead, in speaking of this flint field, calls attention to the fact that no flint in natural deposit is found in the vicinity of Fort Ancient. Hence all this raw material must have been brought from a distance. He notes that the varieties of the flint here found indicated that they were obtained from the quarries of Flint Ridge, Licking county (Ohio) and a flint quarry on the Ohio River in Indiana. In both the Old and New Forts were found several small conical or circular mounds, usually three or four feet high with a base diameter of some twenty feet. Nothing indicative or important was found in any of them. The New Fort presented no such indications of domestic life as did the Old. The latter has therefore been regarded as more exclusively used for military purposes, perhaps a Campus Martius where the warriors were stationed and drilled. Judge **Hosea** thinks:

"Any one examining these works must come to the conclusion that they were erected for defense, and that by a race of men who understood something of the art of war; indeed, much more than can be reasonably attributed to the roving propensities and unstable habits of the American Indian aborigines found upon the continent by the first discoverers of this country. The extent, too, of these works, viewed in the light of military fortifications, proves beyond peradventure that they were raised not for the protection of a tribe more or less numerous, but of a powerful people, raised to war and used to war's alarms; for within these formidable lines there might be congregated, at a moment's notice, fifty or sixty thousand men, with all their materials of war, women, children, and household goods. The Roman legion, we are told, required only a square of seven hundred yards to effect the strongest encampment known to the ancients of Europe and Asia, so that, upon a similar basis, the investment of these fortifications must have been the work of a very formidable body of men indeed, and such as we read of only in the great wars of the Roman emperors with the barbarous hordes that swept from the North, or the masses that were hurled upon each other in the days of the first crusades. The supposition that the works were of a military character, seems to me not only to be the most probable, but the only one, in the absence of any clue, history, or tradition, in the minds of the aborigines, that can be reached."

Judge Force concludes that "Fort Ancient, which would have held a garrison of sixty thousand men, with their families and provisions, was one of a line of fortifications which extended across this state and served to check the incursions of the savages of the north in their descent on the Mound Builders' country. Certainly this structure was a tremendous accomplishment for a primitive people."

Like all the other works of this early people Fort Ancient was unmistakably the product of builders who wrought only with the tools of a stone age. There

Masterpieces of the Mound Builders. 123

were no steam shovels, no derrick scoops to lift the earth and dump it in position — it was "hand made." Not even horses, mules, oxen or wooden sledges facilitated the labor. Though in justice to all authorities it should be noted that there is one unique theory in favor of animal aid. Dr. Frederick Larkin in his "Ancient Man in America" sedately introduces the suggestion that the mastodon, the bones of which are found in Ohio and elsewhere, contemporaneously with those of the Mound Builder, was a "favorite animal and used as a beast of burden" by them. Mr. Larkin then seriously declares it is not difficult for him to believe that those ancient people "tamed that monster of the forest and made him a willing slave to their superior intellectual power." Such being the case he adds: "We can imagine that tremendous teams have been driven to and fro in the vicinity of their great works, tearing up trees by the roots, or marching with their armies into the field of battle amidst showers of poisoned arrows." And why not? The elephants of Alexander and Hannibal did no less centuries before the Christian era.

The late Dr. Edward Orton, president (1898) of the American Association for the Advancement of Science and one of the foremost scientists this country has produced, in an address before the members of the Ohio State Legislature (March, 1898), upon Fort Ancient, said:

124   Masterpieces of the Mound Builders.

"The first point that I make is that the builders of Fort Ancient selected this site for their work with a wide and accurate knowledge of this part of the country.

"You all know of the picturesque location, in the beautiful and fertile valley of the Little Miami, on the table-land that bounds and in places almost overhangs the river, and which is from two hundred to two hundred and fifty feet above the river level. Availing themselves of spurs of the old table-land which were almost entirely cut off by gorges tributary to the river, they ran their earth walls with infinite toil in a tortuous, crenulated line along the margins of the declivities. Where the latter were sharp and precipitous the earth walls were left lighter. Where it became necessary to cross the table-land, or where the slopes were gradual, the walls were made especially high and strong. The eye and brain of a military engineer, a Vauban of the olden time, is clearly seen in all this. We cannot be mistaken in regard to it when we thus find the weak places made strong, and the strong places left as far as possible to their own natural defenses. The openings from the fort, also, lead out in every case to points easily made defensible and that command views from several directions.

"In the second place we cannot be mistaken in seeing in the work of Fort Ancient striking evidences of an organized society, of intelligent leadership, in a word, of strong government. A vast deal of labor was done here and it was done methodically, systematically and with continuity. Here again you must think of the conditions under which the work was accomplished. There were no beasts of burden to share the labors of their owners; the work was all done by human muscles. Baskets full of earth, each containing from a peck to a half bushel, borne on the backs of men or women, slowly built up these walls, which are about four miles in length and which have a maximum height of not less than twenty feet. Reduced to more familiar measurements the earth used in the walls was about 172,000,000 cubic feet.

"But not only were the Mound Builders without the aid of domestic animals of any sort, but they were also without the service of metals. They had no tools of iron; all the picks, hoes and spades that they used were made from chipped flints, and mussel shells from the river must have done the duty of shovels and scrapers. In short, not only was the labor severe and vast, but it was all done in the hardest way.

"Can we be wrong in further concluding that this work was done under a strong and efficient government? Men have always shown that they do not love hard work, and yet hard work was done persistenly here. Are there not evidences on the face of the facts that they were held to their tasks by some strong control?"

He then facetiously suggested there might have been political "bosses" in those days to gather and control the "gang" that built the fort. This latter idea is inimitably suggested in a poem by Mr. Osman C. Hooper, who after visiting the fort, "threw off" the subjoined:

Before Ohio knew a name, a thousand years ago,
A great Cazique stood on the heights and watched Miami's flow;
Tall, straight, majestic as a god, he looked the valley o'er
And heard the hurrying breeze repeat the water's sullen roar.
About him Nature lay full-garbed in leaf and blade and flower,
While he, the Boss, stood clothed upon with little else but power.

Aloof his people stood and gazed — a trembling lot and meek —
And wondered what was holding fast the thought of the Cazique;
Alert to execute his will, they waited his command
And, eager, pressed about him, at the beck'ning of his hand.
"What wouldst thou, master?" they inquired. "Our hands and feet
    are thine,
Command, and thou shalt have it ere the sun again shall shine;"

"What do I want? Look, slaves, and see the beauteous valley
    there,
The bending sky, the teeming soil and all the hues they wear;

Behold the stream that leaps and laughs and roars and then is still;
Look on this bit of heaven dropped within this bowl of hill.
Can ye behold nor guess the wish that in my mind has birth?"
He paused, and loud the thousands cried, "Our lord would have the earth."

"E'en so!" the great Cazique replied. "You boast of what things you
Can do before the morrow's sun drinks, up the morning dew;
But I am lenient, O slaves, and give you just a year
To get the earth and bring it in its wondrous beauty here."

He ceased to speak and waved his hand to bid his people go;
And straight, ten thousand dusky forms, like arrow from a bow,
Sped to the work, each with a bowl and shell for digging fit,
And scratched the earth and took the soil and all that grew in it.

Then, bowl by bowl, they bore the earth to where the monarch stood
And piled it on the height where'er his eye considered good;
They dug and carried, night and day, from brown-leafed fall to fall,
And thus they built upon the height a wondrous earthen wall
Upon their work the monarch looked, then glanced the valley o'er
And marvelled that the earth was there much as it was before.
"Alas!" he cried, "they toil but fail; my wish can never be;
But, if I cannot have the earth, then open, Earth, for me!"

And thus he died, this early Boss of all that mighty clan;
His aim was high like every aim of the Ohio man;
He failed, but still did good and so quite justified the birth
Of that desire within his breast to have and own the earth.